D0396649

NAKED MARKETING
THE BARE ESSENTIALS

ROBERT GREDE

PRENTICE HALL
Englewood Cliffs, New Jersey 07632

Library of Congress Cataloging in Publication Data

Grede, Robert.
    Naked marketing : the bare essentials / Robert Grede.
        p. cm.
    ISBN 0-13-845322-5
    1. Marketing. I. Title.
    HF5415.G657 1997
    658.8—dc21   96-48813
                                   CIP

Printed in the United States of America

10 9 8 7 6 5 4 3 2 1

ISBN 0-13-845322-5

PRENTICE HALL
Career & Personal Development
Englewood Cliffs, NJ 07632
A Simon & Schuster Company

On the World Wide Web at http://www.phdirect.com

Prentice Hall International (UK) Limited, *London*
Prentice Hall of Australia Pty. Limited, *Sydney*
Prentice Hall Canada, Inc., *Toronto*
Prentice Hall Hispanoamericana, S.A., *Mexico*
Prentice Hall of India Private Limited, *New Delhi*
Prentice Hall of Japan, Inc., *Tokyo*
Simon & Schuster Asia Pte. Ltd., *Singapore*
Editora Prentice Hall do Brasil, Ltda., *Rio de Janeiro*

iii

For Cammy and The Nate

Contents

CONTENTS

Introduction

As a marketing consultant, I frequently encounter successful businessmen and women mystified by the role marketing plays in their businesses. They understand the need for it; they understand the results when it is successful; but too often they are confused by how it works.

The truth is, there is no more mystique to marketing than there is to publishing, banking, architecture, or any other profession requiring imagination and intelligent application. "Mystique" is more applicable to things like acupuncture, hypnosis or romance. Marketing is simply a functional specialty, like accounting. All companies in all industries require it in some form or another.

But marketing is more than just "a few ads in the newspaper." Media advertising is but one form of promotion, which is only a small part of an overall marketing program.

Typically, an entrepreneur begins his or her business with a good idea: a better mouse trap, a better way to service clients than his competitors do. And frequently, the founder is a specialist in his or her industry, a good technician, engineer, or designer, but seldom a good marketer for the company.

As the firm grows and competition increases, so grows the need to focus less on the product and more on the customer. The need for this shift in focus is far more evident in today's marketplace than in yesterday's.

Over the past several decades, the marketing function has undergone evolutionary change. During the 1950s and 1960s, marketing was fairly simple. There were fewer product categories and fewer products to choose in each. There were few media vehicles: Television was just coming of age; there were only two dozen major weekly magazines; and FM radio had yet to be heard.

In the 1970s, alternative radio, UHF television, special interest magazines, and the growing sophistication of direct mail brought greater diversity to the marketing mix. Marketers began to specialize and focus on niche markets, on narrow promotional methods, and on specific industries. Successful products spawned product extensions into related categories. New categories developed almost overnight as consumers demanding social change also sought more diversity and uniqueness in their lives.

The 1980s saw the conglomeration of the marketing industry with the advent of mega-agencies such as Sachi & Sachi, McCann Worldwide, and Darcy McManus Benton and Bowles. As a result, many skilled marketing executives who were "downsized" out of the industry formed "boutique" agencies and began specializing in their particular promotional forte. Niche marketing became more focused.

The 1990s offer an even more perplexing array of marketing and promotional options: hundreds of cable television channels; radio stations featuring shock jocks and Christian Coalitions; magazines for every pursuit, profession, or perversion; direct mail techniques that can pinpoint a particular customer by both demographics and lifestyle. And now the Internet!

In response to accelerating change, *guerrilla marketing*, touted as the panacea for small business, fostered the need to get in and get out of the market quickly with as little expense as possible. A noble undertaking, but totally futile if your strategy is ill-planned, your understanding of your customers faulty, or your product message unclear. Guerrilla marketing eventually lost favor as the sole solution for small business and is now merely one tactic among an arsenal available to the astute business owner.

Today, a greater variety of pitfalls awaits the uninitiated. For this reason, before you spend two nickels on marketing, it is important to understand how those nickels should be spent. You need to understand the simple fundamentals of the marketing process. This is not to suggest you, as a small business person, should now concentrate your efforts on learning a whole new field, or abandon your area of expertise. Rather, with an understanding of the *bare essentials* of marketing, you can better plan your strategy and increase your company's sales and profits.

Naked Marketing can help you arrive at that understanding. It explains the marketing function in simple terms and offers real-life examples and effective techniques useful in almost any business. It's a handy tool for anyone who wants to get market-smart quickly and painlessly.

Thank you to Barbara, Avi, David, George, Eric, Mary Jane, Ned, and the folks at PH Direct. Special thanks to Dr. Terry Firkins without whose counsel and creativity this book could not have been written.

¿Que es marketing?

Listen to any ad man, brand manager, or marketing executive for more than a few minutes and you'd think they were talking a foreign language. Forward integration. Backward channeling. Psychographics (conjures up images of Alfred Hitchcock). Gross rating points. Quintile analysis. Post-purchase preferences.

This is marketing?

It needs simplifying. Strip away all that convoluted mumbo jumbo (get down to the bare essentials, if you will) and ask yourself, What is this thing called marketing?

My dictionary defines marketing as "the offering of something for sale." Sounds simple. Take something and sell it.

What if you have a great product, but nobody knows you've got it? Good point. Let's try: "Marketing is the offering of something for sale that we told everybody we had." OK, that works. But what if everybody knows about your great product but they haven't heard of you, and therefore they don't trust you or your company. How about: "Marketing is the offering of something for sale that we told everybody we had with strength and conviction, so everybody trusts us." OK, OK, it's starting to get a little complicated.

Now, what if everybody knows about your great product and trusts you, but can't seem to find it in his store? Add "and we arranged for the physical distribution of the product in a timely manner." And when they do find it, it costs too much. Or it's the wrong size. Or the wrong color. Now we're at "Marketing is the offering of something for sale we told everybody we had with strength and conviction, so that everybody trusts us, and we arranged for the physical distribution of the product in a timely manner at a price everybody could afford in sizes and colors they wanted." Whew.

What if somebody wants to buy your great product on credit? What if your great product breaks? Can somebody get his money back? You begin to get the idea. "Marketing" is complicated, perplexing, mystifying. It has many more aspects than simply the offering of a product for sale. It begins to resemble some sort of unmanageable enigma no one fully understands.

Or does it?

By letting your customers know about your product and making sure it's in the stores when they want to buy it, and by offering it in multiple sizes and colors, aren't you really just trying to give them what they told you they want? Of course you are. You're satisfying needs and wants. That's what marketing is.

Marketing is the satisfaction of needs and wants through the sale of your products or services.

That definition works for all possible contingencies. If your price is perceived to be too high, you really haven't satisfied somebody's need for an affordable product. Likewise, if somebody can't find your product in stores, you haven't satisfied that need, either. If your product could break down, offer a warranty or repair service. If enough somebodies want a larger size, satisfy their desire for your product in a larger size.

Marketing is not simply creating a product and selling it. It's satisfying needs and wants. Figure out what somebody needs and wants and give it to them better and cheaper than your competitors. The best marketers recognize this and reflect it in their advertising:

> *"Have it your way, right away"* (Burger King)
> *"Where do you want to go today?"* (Microsoft)
> *"No dissatisfied customers"* (Ford)

Too often, business owners view marketing as simply the task of creating a product and selling it. Case in point: Contrast Procter & Gamble Company with Union Carbide Corporation.

Union Carbide makes chemicals. Years ago, when I was an advertising executive working on the Glad consumer products business, the top brass told us they had an excess of polyethylene plastic. "Develop some new products that will sell more Glad bags, Rob. Get rid of some of this excess plastics inventory." We all sat around and thought for awhile and eventually developed Handle-Tie Bags. Not because we perceived any consumer demand, but simply because we had excess inventory. (We got lucky and they sold relatively well.)

Procter & Gamble, on the other hand, listens to its field sales representatives, grocery store managers, and the customers themselves. They develop a new product based upon their knowledge of customers' wants and needs. They test it in small markets. Then they spend sinful sums on promotion to create awareness and communicate the benefit (the satisfaction of the needs and wants) to consumers. Procter & Gamble is enormously successful. Union

Carbide no longer has a consumer products division.

Do not confuse needs and wants. They are not the same. Human needs are few: food, clothing, shelter, safety, belonging, esteem (and maybe a good mutual fund). Wants, on the other hand, are desires for specific goods that satisfy a need. A person needs food and wants a cheeseburger, needs clothing and wants an Armani suit, needs shelter and wants a home on the ocean.

Now you may be getting a glimmer of the "alchemy" of marketing. Whoever can turn needs into wants reigns supreme. It's as simple as that. Nevertheless, it presents an intriguing challenge. Critics love to attack marketers who rise to this challenge. They claim marketers create needs. Or that they get people to buy things they don't need. This is a misperception.

Marketers do not create needs. Needs are inherent in our society (food, clothing, shelter, and so forth). Good marketers create wants. They point out how a product satisfies a basic human need. They try to influence desires by making their products attractive, affordable, and readily available. They suggest to consumers that their desire for esteem can be satisfied by a BMW. Or their desire for safety can be satisfied by a Volvo. (Or their desire for belonging can be satisfied by using public transportation.)

Needs exist. Wants can be created. Marketing is simply the act of satisfying those needs and wants.

Not your everyday dictionary definition. But it works.

Knowing your market

So, how do you find out what your customers want?

You do your homework. And in marketing, homework means research. Ask yourself, Who buys my products now? What similarities exist among my customers? Do they all come from the same geographic area? Are they all of the same age group, income bracket, or other demographic? Who else might buy my product? How do I reach those buyers?

As you come to know who your customers are, you must also understand their buying motives, what they really want. Then you can tell them why they should buy your products instead of your competitors'.

PRIMARY VERSUS SECONDARY RESEARCH

Okay, let's begin. There are two types of research: *primary* and *secondary*. What's the difference? Let's use some examples. When you were in high school and you had to write a term paper on China, or on the mating habits of the Borneo lizard, you probably didn't fly to China or purchase and observe a thousand lizards. That would be *primary* research.

Instead, you looked up the information in a book. That's *secondary* research. Lots cheaper. Secondary research means gathering information from existing sources, stuff that others have already compiled.

Industry trade groups and trade magazines offer heaps of secondary research on your industry. And it's free for the asking. Every industry has one or more trade organizations. Even if you're not a member, because you might be someday, they are often more than willing to fill your "In" basket with a mountain of information (along with a membership application), such as statistics on buying and selling habits, peak selling months, or a geographical breakdown of the highest consumption areas for various product categories. Trade magazines often publish lists of the sales people, manufacturers' representatives, and wholesale distributors for your industry. Just ask.

While secondary research is cheaper and easier, there may not be any information that somebody else has already compiled about who your specific customers are, or what they want. In that case, you need to consider a little primary research. Primary research is more difficult because it means doing it yourself, compiling information through testing, interviews, or questionnaires. Don't worry. It need not be expensive. Not if you ask the right questions of the right people. What kinds of questions? Here are a few thought-starters:

1. What is the name of our product or service?

2. What does this name mean to you?

3. How often do you purchase this type of product?

4. What is the primary reason you purchase the brand you do?

5. What are the strengths/advantages of this product?

6. What are the competitors' strengths/advantages over this product?

7. If you believe that a company can offer only two out of three—quality, service, or price—which two would you say best characterize this product?

Who do you ask?

Start in your own company. Ask the most senior employee (after yourself). He has stored several megabytes of industry knowledge in his cranium over the years. But be careful. That knowledge may be based upon data that's ten years old, when he was last out in the field. And customers don't care what your company contributed to the industry ten years ago, or even ten days ago. Customers deal with now, and so must we. So listen for the facts and ignore the age-old opinions.

Other sources in your company include sales representatives, the folks closest to your customers; your receptionist, who talks to customers every day; your customer service department for the same reason; and even shipping clerks, the ones reading the shipping labels on a daily basis.

Salespeople
Sales representatives are loaded with information. The good ones know why your customers buy your products and what motivates them to buy from you over the competition. The sales rep can also be a source for new product opportunities. Just be careful never to ask a "yes" or "no" question. For example, don't ask your rep, "Uncover any new uses for our product lately?" It's too easy to say no. He'll just scratch his chin for a moment and then slowly shake his head.

Better to appeal to the ego. I once asked a sales rep why she sold so few of a particular product. Stung by my implied criticism, she countered that it took too long to sell those penny-ante little products. By the time customers decided what to buy, she had spent ten minutes selling a five-dollar item. She went on to criticize the company for not prepacking an assortment of the best-selling products. Then she could sell $50 worth in half the time. It was, of course, a brilliant idea, and we all wondered why nobody had thought of it before, and the company did just as she suggested and everybody was happy, including the customers, but especially the saleswoman.

Shipping Clerks

Shipping clerks are aware of the ultimate destination of your products and can alert you to entirely new markets. One of our shipping clerks once pointed out that he was shipping dozens of a particular type of watch to a hospital. Investigation revealed the hospital's school of nursing used them because their large face and sweep second hand were perfect for reading a patient's pulse. Bingo! A whole new market for our watches: schools of nursing.

Customers

The best way to know what your customers want is to ask them. Periodically, all your existing customers should receive a "How are we doing?" letter. Give them a chance to sound off, register any complaints or concerns, and offer suggestions for improvement. You will be amazed at the benefits: head off problems before they become problems; learn how you stack up against your competitors. And the suggestions your customers offer may lead to additional sales or even to a new product opportunity. Best of all, your customers will feel better because they have the sense that you care about their needs.

ADVERTISING RESEARCH

Another good way to find out what your customers want is by testing your advertising. For example, if you're sending out a direct-mail piece and you are undecided about whether to use Headline A touting the dependability of your product or Headline B boasting the lowest price, try both. Send one to half your mailing list, half to the other, and watch the results. Your customers will tell you which is more important.

Retail store managers understand this concept all to well. Their reward (or punishment) is immediate. If they have a powerful ad, they'll see the noses of eager consumers pressed up against the doors before the store opens in the morning. If not, they had better write a good one fast or be accountable to their buyers, merchandise managers, and maybe even the president of the store.

Test your media the same way. Run the same ad in two or more publications using a different code on each return card or a different toll-free number in each ad (or some means of differentiating among responses). Then watch the results. Whichever one pulls the most responses per dollar invested becomes your media of choice for the future.

We ran a coupon advertisement for a chain of dry cleaning stores in three different publications. Each coupon featured the same offer, but each had a different code so we could count the redemptions. After a few weeks, we realized one newspaper, the one with the biggest circulation, pulled better than the others. However, its advertising space cost twice as much as the newspaper that pulled second best. After we divided the cost by the total redemptions, the second-best newspaper proved the most cost effective.

Don't test both your ad message and your media at the same time. It will only lead to confusion. If we had varied the coupon offer, we would never know whether the coupon which redeemed the most was because of the offer or the newspaper we had used.

Market research can reveal untold opportunities for new products, provide a wealth of knowledge about your competitors, and help you better understand your customers' needs and wants. Research for some can seem tedious or even intimidating. Not to worry. The remainder of this book is devoted to providing you with the tools and aptitude needed to become an effective marketer for your business. A major part of your understanding will come from grasping the idea of marketing as a process. As a matter of fact, that is our next subject.

How to develop a plan

Marketing is a process. Given our obsession with results, we are often misled into seeing our business as a product. But examine the phrase "business we do" or "doing business." "Doing" is an action verb. It signifies that something progresses over time. It is a process.

THE FOUR P'S

Think of this process as a big recipe. Into it go all the ingredients that cause customers to buy your product or service over somebody else's. The name, the package, where you sell it, how you advertise it, your warranty—all are part of your recipe for success.

Experts put these ingredients, these marketing variables, into four categories called the Four P's:

Product	**P**lace	**P**romotion	**P**rice
Name	Inventory	Advertising	Discounts
Packaging	Channels	Publicity	Credit terms
Sizes	Locations	Sales promotion	Warranties
Features	Transport	Personal selling	Returns

As a marketer, you must choose which ingredients best fit your needs. You and your competitors share a common problem: a limited marketing budget. When you shop for your marketing variables, you can spend only so much on each ingredient. Good marketing decisions are based upon estimates of the net revenue produced by investment in these ingredients. Put all your budget in packaging and you'll have a product that really stands out on store shelves, but no money to promote it. Meanwhile, your competitor may have used her budget to offer more features or more sizes. Or she may have devoted some of her budget to advertising, some to promotions, some to discounts. Ultimately, she attracts more customers. The secret, then, is to balance the marketing variables and emphasize those that are most important to your customers. This starts with good planning.

There are three ways to develop a plan in your company. One is the top-down approach (often called Theory X management, in which it is assumed employees dislike work and need to be directed) in which the boss sets goals and allocates the budget accordingly. The bottom-up approach (Theory Y: employees like their work and are more committed if they participate in the running of the company) has employees setting their own goals based upon the best they think they can do. The best approach is often a combination (Theory Z: goals down, plans up) in which top management sets goals and the employees are responsible for developing plans designed to achieve those goals.

Planning is essential, yet often meets with resistance. This opposition is based upon (1) the sense that there are "more important" things to do; (2) the perception that planning is simply "busy work" and not useful; and (3) reluctance to commit to goals in a rapidly changing environment. As owner, you must emphasize the importance of planning. If the boss isn't sold on planning, nobody else will be either. To get everybody else behind the idea of planning, you, in a sense, need a plan for selling employees on the benefits of planning.

Here are some of the benefits of planning:

- Encourages thinking ahead in a systematic manner
- Sharpens the company's focus
- Prepares for unforeseen developments
- Leads to better coordination of company efforts
- Helps develop performance standards
- Inspires a sense of commitment to the planning process

THE MARKETING PLAN

What does a marketing plan look like? Despite myriad variations, every good plan has certain basic elements:

- Outline or Table of Contents
- Executive Summary
- Situation Analysis
- Objectives
- Strategies
- Tactics
- Budget

Outline
The outline is the headings of each section with page numbers (remember to include page numbers—without them, anybody reading your plan is lost).

Executive Summary
Begin your marketing plan with a one-page summary of the circumstances and principal recommendations contained in the plan. This allows everyone to grasp quickly the main thrust of the plan and then lets them read further in search of the information most critical to his or her part in it.

Situation Analysis

This section describes where your company stands at that moment in time. It includes background on past sales, major competitors, and explanations of recent sales and profit results. It should also feature a forecast for the industry, including opportunities and threats (for example, the government is about to slap a tariff on foreign-made gimcracks, or the cost of raw materials is expected to double over the next year) and some mention of the company's strengths and weaknesses versus the competition.

Objectives

Every company has objectives. They are simply a matter of deciding where you want to be and when you want to get there.

- Is the purpose of your marketing plan to launch a new product or line of products? If so, your objective might read, "Achieve 10 percent market share within the first 12 months of product launch."

- Is the purpose of your marketing plan to boost revenue from existing products? Your objective then might read, "Increase revenue 12 percent from our existing line of products over the next six months while maintaining current profit margins."

Notice that each objective is quantifiable and features a limited time frame. Make your objectives definable and measurable. It lets all involved know how they're doing along the way.

Not all objectives, however, need to be quantifiable. For example, many of my clients complain that they have to spend too much time wrestling with alligators and cannot spend enough time draining the swamp. One of their objectives becomes: "Spend less time putting out fires and more time planning and administering." This objective is nonspecific, and, therefore, difficult to measure.

Strategies

Strategies are the things you need to do to accomplish your objectives. If your objective is where you want your company to be, the strategy is the route you need to take to get there. For example, if the objective is to increase sales revenue, your strategies might be one or more of the following:

- Increase the average price on all units
- Increase overall sales volume
- Sell more of the higher-priced units
- Any combination of these

What happens if your market changes? Avoid a tendency for tunnel vision by making a list of alternative marketing strategies. Think outside the box. It will keep you from being locked into one way of thinking about your market so you won't miss any opportunities.

Each of these strategies may be broken down further. Sales volume can be increased through increasing your market share or growth in the market itself. If you dominate a market, you may wish to influence the growth of that market. When RCA was the dominant manufacturer of television sets, they encouraged consumers to own more than one, thus increasing the overall size of the market. As the market grew, so did their sales.

Tactics

Entrepreneurs often confuse strategies and tactics. "Develop a brochure to send to new prospects" is not a strategy. "Increase awareness among potential customers" is a strategy. The brochure is simply a tactic for implementing that strategy. Whereas strategies establish a broad outline of how you want to achieve your objectives, tactics are specific actions. A brochure is a tactic; an ad in the newspaper is a tactic; promotional pens or T-shirts with your name and logo on them are tactics. In other words, while objectives and strategies are conceptual visions, tactics are the tangible fulfillment of those visions.

Budget

Of course, each tactic has a price. Add up all that you plan to use and you know what your budget must be to achieve your goals. But what if your tactics are beyond your budget? What if you have designed a plan with so many powerful and potentially effective tactics that your whole company isn't worth that much? Simple. You prioritize. Use what I call "Net Revenue Projection." I know, it's one of those terms that almost makes your eyes glaze over and your mind start to wander. But until I think of a better name for it, this moniker will have to do. What it means is that each tactic needs a profit and loss statement. Like this:

Net Revenue Projection for Tactic #1

Projected additional revenue using tactic #1	$12,000
Cost of additional goods sold	(8,000)
Gross additional revenue	$ 4,000
Cost of tactic #1	(3,000)
Net revenue	$ 1,000

Let's say your restaurant usually sells 1,200 fish fries on a typical Friday night. With drinks and desserts, your average check is around $12 and your cost of food and paper goods is about $4 per person. Now, say you're considering putting an ad in your local paper. The ad will cost $750 and you estimate it will bring in 150 new customers on Friday night. Should you run the ad? Or should you investigate some other tactic? To answer that question, estimate the Net Revenue Projection.

Projected additional revenue (150 fish fries @ $12)	$1,800
Cost of additional food and paper (150 @ $4)	(600)
Gross additional revenue	$1,200
Cost of ad	(750)
Net Revenue	$ 450

In the first example, an investment of $3,000 yields a return of $1,000, or 33 percent. When weighed against the risk of tactic #1 working up to projections, this may not be a good investment. In the restaurant example, your ad cost $750 and returned $450, a 60-percent return on your investment. Even if your ad only pulls in 100 new customers, you still make a small profit.

Projected additional revenue (100 fish fries @ $12)	$1,200
Cost of additional food and paper (100 @ $4)	(400)
Gross additional revenue	$ 800
Cost of ad	(750)
Net Revenue	$ 50

The risk is small; the potential rewards are great. Go with the ad.

After determining the Net Revenue Projection for each tactic, it becomes easy to eliminate those tactics from your marketing plan that are either too expensive or too risky. But don't be too hasty in your assessment. Some tactics may not directly contribute to an increase in revenue. They may, however, be necessary to the support of other tactics. (For examples, see the following abbreviated sample Marketing Plan. Use it to help develop yours [or use it as a comparison when presented one by your advertising agency].)

Ultimately, your entire marketing budget is a projected profit-and-loss statement. On the revenue side are the forecasted number of new units that will be sold as a result of your combined tactics, and the average net price. On the expense side are the cost of production, distribution, and the marketing costs. The difference is the net profit of implementing this plan. (For more about budget, see Chapter 13.)

What would happen if you spent nothing at all on marketing?

If you spend no money on marketing, you may lose market share, and profit might decrease. Be sure to consider this lost revenue when making your Net Revenue Projections. For example, let's say you estimate that if you do no marketing, sales will decline and profits will be off $2,000. You also estimate that if you spend $50,000 on marketing, you will realize a profit increase of $4,000. So, your net revenue is really $6,000, the $4,000 profit plus the $2,000 you'd have lost if you had done no marketing.

Okey Doke, Inc.
MARKETING PLAN

EXECUTIVE SUMMARY

Okey Doke, Inc., is a plastic injection molding firm with annual sales of $2 million. This plan was developed to provide opportunities for increasing sales 40 percent or more over the next three years. The company will expand its sales territory and attract new customers through direct mailing, publicity, and the personal selling efforts of independent manufacturers' representatives.

SITUATION ANALYSIS

Okey Doke, Inc., uses technologically advanced plastic molding equipment capable of unattended operation to provide just-in-time service to clients in Minnesota, Wisconsin, and Michigan's Upper Peninsula. Sales have been flat over the past two years due to a highly price-competitive market, but have experienced steady growth the four previous years. The company has an excellent reputation and typically turns 15 percent of quote requests into customers. Opportunities exist for expansion to Illinois and Iowa due to higher price points and fewer competitors in this region.

OBJECTIVES

1. Increase sales 40 percent over the next three years while maintaining 20-percent profit margins or better.

2. Retain current mix of customers so no one customer represents more than 20 percent of sales.

3. Relieve Joe Dokes, owner, of the burden of sales, allowing him more time for administration and quality control.

STRATEGIES

1. In all promotion materials, present clear, consistent image of quality and service to target market.

2. Hire Independent Manufacturers' Sales Organization(s) to relieve Dokes of sales responsibilities.

3. Expand to markets beyond current geographic region of Minnesota, Wisconsin and the Upper Peninsula.

4. Provide ample sales support for sales representatives.

5. Develop training programs for sales representatives designed to encourage loyalty and enhance service image of firm.

6. Respond to quote requests faster.

TACTICS

1. *Seek out, retain, and train independent sales representatives* (at a 10-percent commission rate) to cover the territory of Illinois and Iowa, which will increase customer base by 120 percent.

2. *Purchase CAD/CAM design system.* Customer research indicates it is important to return quote requests promptly. Current average turnaround time is ten days. Okey Doke will cut this time to five days by purchasing a CAD/CAM design system and using computer-dedicated fax lines to return quote requests promptly.

3. *Hold annual sales meeting.* The additional sales representatives require training and a sense of "team spirit." An annual meeting will have elements of both work (presentation of sales support materials, shop floor tours, supplier tours, motivational speaker and so forth) and play (golf outing, baseball game, barbecue picnic and so forth).

4. *Develop new brochure.* Feedback from the field indicates a need for a more detailed brochure that can be used as a direct mailing prior to a sales call, a "leave behind" at the sales call, or as a follow-up to a customer contact. The brochure will accurately reflect the quality and service image of the company while outlining the firm's capabilities, manufacturing specifications and equipment, competitive advantages, and subsequent benefits to the customers.

5. *Obtain magazine reprints.* Use high-quality reprints of company's trade journal advertisements for distribution by sales representatives, in mailings, and at trade shows.

6. *Direct mailing.* Purchase prospective customer mailing lists targeting by ZIP Code (Illinois, Iowa), Standard Industry Classification (SIC) code, and sales (over $10 million but less than $1 billion). Develop mailing designed to attract

5 percent or better prospect inquiries, of which 15 percent will become customers. Provide lists to sales representatives and notify them which portion of the list will be mailed and when.

7. *Publicity.* The company will use its public relations agency to develop articles of interest to the industry while portraying the firm in a positive light. Emphasis will be placed on publications in the Midwest, particularly in Illinois, Iowa, and Wisconsin.

BUDGET

1. *Hire new independent manufacturers sales organization(s).* An additional independent sales organization will expand the area served by the firm, thus increasing sales. It will also serve to relieve the owner of the burden of sales in the new territories.

Projected additional revenue	
(40% of sales by third year)	$800,000
Cost of goods sold (@ 20% profit margin)	(640,000)
Gross additional revenue	$160,000
Sales cost (10% commission)	(80,000)
Net revenue projection	$ 80,000

Cost: $500 for meals and entertainment

2. *Respond to quote requests faster.* New CAD/CAM software will shorten turnaround time on quote requests, eliminating sales lost (estimated at 5 percent) due to slow service. This tactic supports the field sales force in their efforts to provide the best service, and it is consistent with the firm's efforts to enhance its service image.

Projected additional revenue (5% of sales)	$100,000
Cost of goods sold (@ 20% profit margin)	(80,000)
Gross additional revenue	$ 20,000
CAD/CAM software and training	(8,000)
Net revenue projection	$ 12,000

Cost: $8,000 for CAD/CAM software and training

3. *Hold annual sales meeting.* (No net revenue projection.) This tactic is necessary to provide training and support for sales force.

Cost ($1,000 per year for three years): $ 3,000

4. *Develop new brochure.* (No net revenue projection.) A new brochure is necessary to provide support for the sales force and direct mail efforts.

Cost (3,500 @ $0.40 each): $ 1,400

5. *Obtain magazine reprints.* (No net revenue projection.) Reprints further support the field sales force and serve as promotional pieces for a variety of uses.

6. *Direct mailing.*

Projected additional revenue (5% of 2,500 mailing @ 15% closing rate and $2,000 average new order)	$37,500
Cost of goods sold (@ 20% profit margin)	(30,000)
Gross additional revenue	$ 7,500
Sales cost (list, mailing piece and postage @ $ 0.90 each)	(2,250)
Net revenue projection	$ 5,250

7. *Publicity.* (No net revenue projection.) Publicity provides a credible forum for creating awareness and enhancing the firm's reputation for quality and service.

Establish an image for your firm

With some of the mechanics of planning behind us, we can begin to focus on subjects related to the long-term prosperity of your company. Image is one of the most crucial. The clothes your company wears *are* important. They project a sense of who you are and where you're going.

Here's an old saying I just made up: "Quality, Service, or Price—pick any two out of three."

Q, S, & P

It happens all the time. Your customer wants it yesterday; he wants it perfect; and he wants to pay next to nothing for it. "Oh, and can you deliver it?" Relax, he's supposed to make demands. After all, he's your customer. He wants exceptional quality, fast service, and low price, and it's your job to see that he gets all three. Or is it? Do that for very long, you'll be out of business.

Choosing which two out of three best suits your company is critical to establishing your image in the marketplace.

Think of it as a big equation:

$$Q + S = P$$

If your quality is high and your service is excellent, your price must be high, too.

If your quality is high, but your service is slow, your price should be lower:

$$\mathbf{Q} + S = P$$

And if you sell second-quality goods, no matter how good your service, your price must reflect the quality of the merchandise:

$$Q + \mathbf{S} = P$$

For example, Chef Pierre's Cafe Francais features escargot and filet mignon and impeccable service. But Chef Pierre may cost you your credit limit.

A McDonald's restaurant, on the other hand, offers quick service and a low price. But their food can't compare with Chef Pierre's. If Chef Pierre tried to offer great quality, impeccable service, and match McDonald's prices too, he'd soon be out of business.

Chef Pierre doesn't advertise low prices. Nor does McDonald's pretend to have the best food in town. Neither tries to be something it is not in the minds of its customers. Neither tries to project an image inconsistent with their choice of Q, S, & P. Yet both do very well simply by being the best at their two out of three.

Don't get me wrong. Sometimes you have to offer all three to keep a longstanding customer happy. If your best customer suddenly has an emergency and needs your best product at a low-ball price and he needs it immediately, you can't take the chance of losing him to a competitor. So you give him all three, even if it means you lose money on the transaction.

If you do offer all three, however—quality, service, and price—you had better have confidence you can make up for any loss on that customer's next orders.

By being flexible, some companies are able to create the impression that their customers receive all three. They can adapt their pricing, or service, or even the quality of their product according to their customers' needs. In effect, they choose the two that best suit the situation.

A client in the printing business uses this method effectively. His firm offers all three, but only two at a time. "If the customer wants a new brochure fast and perfect," says Dale Wilson, president of Alternative Graphics in Santa Barbara, California, "we may charge extra for the rush service. Likewise, if he wants perfect quality but can afford to wait for awhile, I can beat anybody's price." Wilson adds that he seldom offers the other two, low price and fast service, together. "Quality will suffer, and we're not willing to compromise on that. It puts our company's reputation in jeopardy."

Any firm that offers only one of the three will soon be discovered by its customers. They probably won't be customers for very long. A low price will not make up for both poor quality and lousy service. Nor will the best product be sold at a high price if the service is too slow.

Likewise, there are dangers in trying to provide all three. Trying to be too much to too many can stretch your firm's abilities and resources.

An acquaintance who repaired boat engines offered the same quality parts as his competitors and matched his competitor's prices dollar for dollar. But he also provided far superior service, painting the inside of the motor housings, degreasing all the parts before assembly, and generally tidying up his customers' engines for aesthetic reasons as well as peak performance. Unfortunately, all this additional labor took time for which he had to pay his employees. His costs were higher; his quality was the same as his competition. And his prices were the same or lower. His customers loved him, and he lost money on every one. Last season was his last season in business.

When you choose your two, be sure your customers know which two. If you choose quality and service, tell them that although you can't always guarantee the lowest price, you sell only the best merchandise and will bend over backward to serve their needs. So long as you fulfill your promise of quality and service, your customers can appreciate your need to charge a little more. Or if a customer knows she's getting the lowest price in town on a top-of-the-line washer and dryer, she won't be so disappointed when she can't find a salesperson immediately.

Quality, service, or price. Pick any two out of three. Then communicate that image to your customers and prospects. After choosing your Q, S, & P position, which amounts to knowing your company's mission in the marketplace, you are now ready to engage in the literary task of writing a mission statement.

THE MISSION STATEMENT

It is said, "If you don't know where you're going, any road will get you there." That's why every company, including yours, needs a mission statement. It defines who you are as a company, sets the mood, articulates the corporate culture, and helps perpetuate favorable work methods. In short, it serves as a guide on the long road to success.

Externally, the mission statement is a beacon in the fog. It provides management a focus when they are faced with uncertainties due to corporate expansion, competitive harassment, or industry deregulation. Internally, it demonstrates leadership and helps to inspire employees.

For your organization to have a mission statement, it must have a mission, one by which you probably operate your business intuitively, one that your employees may or may not share, one that now needs articulating. Writing a formal statement doesn't just voice this unspoken mission, it endorses it as company policy.

There are many benefits to having a written statement. If your employees live by your guiding principles, they don't have to run to the rule book every time they make a decision. They can look at the mission statement to remind them what their boss would have them do. This can avoid a lot of annoying meetings.

Avoiding annoying meetings is just one reason mission statements are popular among large companies. Boston-based consultants Bain & Co. recently surveyed the use of mission statements. More than nine out of every ten *Fortune 500* firms use them. They are more widely used than any other management tool. Why? Because the cost is small, and they work.

Big companies use mission statements in different ways. Some are fanatic about spreading the missionary zeal. The Ritz-Carlton Hotel displays its "Credo" at meetings and expects its employees to be able to recite it upon request. Bob Galvin, former chairman and CEO of Motorola Inc., required employees to carry a wallet-sized card of the company's mission statement and occasionally asked them to show it.

At Leo Burnett Advertising Agency, we had to know both Leo's mission statement ("Our primary function in life is to produce the best advertising in the world, bar none.") and motto ("Reach for the stars. You may not always get one, but you won't come up with a handful of mud either.").

Many managers use mission statements in training. Arthur D. Little Inc. uses its "Mission and Guiding Principles" as an orientation guide for new employees. McDonald's Quality Service Cleanliness and Value (QSCV) is an integral part of the training of new hires.

That is not to say *any* mission statement is better than no mission statement at all. Some mission statements are unrealistic. Boeing Company's fundamental goal of achieving 20-percent average annual return on stockholder's equity, or Earth Care Paper's mission to "improve the world" both seem a bit wishful.

Some are unclear. General Electric's "Boundaryless . . . Speed . . . Stretch" or Ball Corporation's pledge to maintain high levels of social responsibility sound good, but leave the reader asking, "What does it mean?"

Dexter Corporation uses just one long, run-on sentence:

To be recognized as an important and environmentally responsive specialty materials company that derives superior growth and returns from quality products and responsive services based on proprietary technology and operating excellence that provides genuine benefit to customers worldwide, rewards talented and dedicated employees, and satisfies shareholder expectations.

Huh?

Some are as folksy as the founder. In 1926, I. J. Cooper expressed his Cooper Tire & Rubber Co. creed as "Good merchandise, fair play, and a square deal." Banc One Corp. uses the words of its chairman, John B. McCoy: "We'll deal with you straight, no fluff and no excuses . . ."

The U.S. Air Force uses a mission statement as simple and direct as a B-52: "To defend the United States through control and exploitation of air and space."

Your company may not be entrusted with the control of air and space, but a mission statement is no less essential. It forces management to think strategically, something too often overlooked amid the day-to-day crises facing most small business owners. A mission statement also inspires employees to follow the guiding principles endorsed by their leader. It can even serve as a sales tool when used to reinforce a key product benefit.

Developing a mission statement for your company need not take a lot of time and energy. Usually, you as founder or president simply need to sit down after a long day of arduous alligator wrestling and meaningless meetings and sketch a few words on paper to remind yourself why you decided to go into business in the first place.

During a relaxed moment, if you can find one, reflect on why you decided to be a small business owner. If you can recapture that inspiration, your mission statement will most likely turn out inspiring. Because experts agree, the most effective mission statement inspires. To inspire, it must galvanize employees. It must grab their attention, motivate them to work harder, smarter, in words that ring true for today and for tomorrow. Eloquence is not essential. Any divorced person will tell you there is no mission statement more movingly phrased than the traditional wedding vows, or more difficult to live up to.

Also, avoid corporatese. A credo like Dexter's won't galvanize anyone outside the legal department. Keep it simple and direct. Phrase it as if you were talking to a friend.

Here's a good way to start. Answer in 50 words or less: Why are you in business? Why this product? Why these customers? Pick the principles you live by. Write them down. Then build your credo from the principles you want your employees to emulate.

Now follow through. Once you've written it, use your mission statement. Share it with your employees. Post it around the office. Display it at meetings.

Distribute it to customers and suppliers. Print it on your letterhead, purchase orders, and invoices. Use it as a direct mailing to all your customers and potential customers. Enclose a copy and a cover letter explaining how it was written and how you intend to live up to it today and in the future. Its omnipresence will imprint itself on the mind of your company. It will become your company's character, its IMAGE. It will influence every facet of your business. This includes your marketing and advertising, which communicates your mission and image to your customers.

THE TOTAL APPROACH

To understand the connection between image and advertising, we first need to look at two types of advertising. One promotes a company's *product* (or service); the other promotes the *corporate* image.

Product advertising is designed to sell a particular product for a limited time. Examples include low 3.9-percent financing on your new car through the end of the month or get a free toaster with your deposit of $1,000 or more, while supplies last. The Buy-a-Kiddy-Meal-get-a-free-toy ad you see on TV is a promotion designed to sell a specific product for a limited period of time. That's product advertising.

Advertisers who use only product advertising expect each ad to result in an immediate increase in sales of the product or service advertised. But product advertising alone is less effective if the customer is unfamiliar with the company offering the product or if the customer does not have a clearly defined sense of the product image. Most large advertisers increase the effectiveness of their product advertising by supplementing it with *corporate image advertising*.

This type of advertising goes by many names: image, identity, the "big idea." It is intended to portray the company in a favorable light. It is intended to build positive feelings for your company's prod-

ucts. It encompasses the set of beliefs your customers associate with your company. The better the
image, the greater the trust in your products.

That warm, fuzzy little-boy-about-to-meet-his-
baby-brother-enjoys-an-order-of-fries-with-Dad TV
spot sells image: McDonald's fries are great when
you have to discuss life's little problems. The advertisement's objective is to have you, the viewer, associate traditional family values with McDonald's. It
isn't necessarily intended to sell french fries specifi-
cally.

Those popular TV spots for IBM featuring subtitled
scenes of actors in exotic locales discussing the
global problem-solving capabilities of IBM computers are not designed to sell a specific computer.
Rather, they create an *image*. They portray the company as hero.

That's all well and good for the big boys, but unfortunately, a small business doesn't always have the
budget to execute separate product and corporate
image advertising. So it is all the more important to
ensure your advertising does both.

I call this the *Total Approach*. It begins with consistency from one marketing effort to the next; for
instance, a uniform design relationship. Same color
scheme, same logo art, same tag line. Same general
look and "feel" to all your marketing efforts. Even if
a potential customer skims over your magazine or
newspaper ad without reading it carefully, the tag
line or corporate symbol may register. The more
consistent your marketing efforts have been, the
more likely this subliminal association will be.

The most important factor in the Total Approach is
make it easy for your customers to recognize your
product at a glance. United has the friendly skies;
McDonald's has the golden arches; Keebler has
elves. Each identifies the product or service quickly
and efficiently. Each jars the memory and alerts a
potential customer to the product being advertised.

The first step to achieving this power of association is to define your position in the market. Differentiate your firm or your product or service from your competitors'. Are your firm's products the most reliable, the least expensive, the highest quality, backed by the friendliest service? Your position should help customers know the real difference between you and your competitors so that they can match their needs to the one that can be of most value to them.

Then, pick a visual image that represents your market position. For example, the Harris Bank in Chicago uses a lion to represent strength. That corporate symbol appears on their buildings, their signage, their brochures, and all their advertising. Dawn Dishwashing Liquid is positioned as a grease cutter. Each Dawn TV commercial ends with a drop of liquid dispelling grease in a pan and the tag line, "Dawn takes away grease." Simple, memorable, effective.

Unfortunately, some companies adopt an ambiguous image. Like a politician who is running for office, they seek to be different things to different market segments. Bad move. They succeed only in confusing their customers. Whether it's a newspaper ad, brochure, or the sign on your front door, use the Total Approach to establish instant recognition and a consistent image for your firm and its products. Consistent image will lead to consistent profits.

NAME AWARENESS

Once you have clearly defined your image, promote it to customers. Fix it in their minds. It is critical that your customers and prospects know who you are and what you stand for so that you are among their choices when it comes time to make a purchase. Ask people why they bought a product, and invariably they respond "Because I heard of it." That's name awareness.

Customers of all types—whether selling business to business or to consumers—often buy products simply because they are familiar with the name. How do you acquire name awareness? Start with a good name. Make it easy to pronounce and spell. Henry Bloch and his brother spell their company H&R Block.

Then, repeat the name of your company or product wherever and whenever you can. Put it on your purchase orders, invoices, and other mailings to suppliers and customers. Outfit your employees in T-shirts and jackets with your company name and logo on them. Get a sign for the side of your car. Sponsor a softball team, and be sure the team wears uniforms with your name on them. Frequent advertising, conspicuous signage, regular mailings, and positive publicity in the newspaper or other media will translate into "Because I heard of it."

One of the best ways to assure name awareness: Use a multitude of tactics across a variety of media simultaneously. For instance, every major automobile company simultaneously runs TV and radio spots, mails brochures and product announcements, and gets wide coverage for its new cars in trade magazines and local newspapers. The company doesn't expect you to run right out and buy a new car today. It just wants you to include it on your short list when you're ready to trade in that old DeSoto for a new set of wheels.

Make each ad work harder for you by supplementing it with other marketing tactics—newspaper ads, radio spots, publicity, brochures, newsletters, and direct mailings, all timed to your industry's biggest trade show. Suddenly deluged by your company message, your customers and prospects will begin to sense a leader in the marketplace. They hear your name on the radio, read a story about your company in the newspaper, then see your ad in a trade magazine. You can bet they'll be more prone to read your brochure when it lands on their desk. They'll also be more apt to call on you rather than on a competitor when it's time to buy, and your profits will begin speaking for themselves.

COMMUNCATING YOUR IMAGE TO CUSTOMERS

So, you've defined who you are with your mission statement, used that to define your company's image, and now you have decided to create awareness for your company through a variety of media. Which media are best? Who designs your ad campaign? Who writes the words? Who produces it? Who? The answer is either you, or an outside agency.

Let's consider *you* first. Anyone can open an advertising agency. You don't have to pass a written test or apply for any special license. So, why not you? You run a small business now. Why not add advertising to your list of responsibilities? Lots of small-business people do. With no "entry barrier" to becoming their own advertising agency, they see some of the advertising on television or in magazines and think, "Hey, I can write better mindless drivel than that." On top of that, ad agencies mark up everything they produce as much as 20 percent, they charge 15-percent commission on media, and they don't know nearly so much about your product or industry as you do. Who needs them?

You do. Here are three reasons why:

1. An agency takes the burden of the production process off your hands and makes sure everything is done right. Agencies mark up production because they earn it. You may know how to write compelling, persuasive ads; or you may know where to contact a good illustrator; you may even know how to spec type, judge a good chromolin, or read a printer's blueprint (or van dyke). But it's not likely you know how to do all of these things.

2. You generally pay the same price for media whether you use an agency or not. Better to let a professional do the planning and buying for you.

3. The pros at ad agencies are masters of their specific craft. Your lawyer or your accountant will

never know your industry as well as you do. They know law and accounting. Likewise, your ad agency knows advertising and how to apply it to your business.

Choosing an Ad Agency

You have three choices when delegating the advertising responsibility:

1. A full-service agency
2. An advertising "boutique"
3. A consulting service

The full-service agency is ideal if you need full service. Full service includes marketing research, media planning and buying services, idea concepting, copywriting, layout and design work, and production services. Big full-service agencies generate some of the best creative ideas in the world. Their advice and counsel may be worth every penny you pay for it.

Unfortunately, "big" agencies like to work for "big" clients. Their best people work on accounts that generate lots of income. They may do great work on full-page ads in *Sports Illustrated*. But a quarter page in *Control Engineering* is just not their cup of gin. So your account gets sloughed off to the new kid in the agency. You may like the sound of saying you're with a big agency, but the benefit can often end there.

If you need a full-service agency, go for one that suits your size. Look for a small, personalized operation headed by one or two pros, experienced advertising professionals who work on each account themselves. They will work closely with you and get to know your manufacturing, marketing, and sales needs. They can serve as a source of experience and advertising wisdom. In effect, you pay for their talent, not for agency overhead.

Then again, if you don't need all the services of a full-service agency, you don't need to pay for them.

Use a boutique agency. It's an a la carte approach that often works well for smaller businesses. A boutique agency is usually founded by one or two professionals with specific skills. They specialize in one or two functions. That way, you don't pay the overhead for services you don't use. You pay only for the services you need.

For example, you have a dynamite ad that ran in your local paper and generated lots of sales. Now you want to expand to other markets. You may only need a media buying service to plan and buy space in the newspapers in your chosen markets. Or, your industry has only one trade magazine that is read by everyone. And you want to continue advertising in it exclusively. You may only need a creative boutique to design and execute a few innovative ads that will pull in customers.

The third option is the Independent Consultant. This is usually a single-person operation. Their overhead is low, and you can count on their close attention. The independent consultant frequently works with a loose affiliation of similar single-person operations to provide a complete range of services.

Sometimes, they can lack depth of knowledge in more than one or two functions. And they may try to do too much, rather than calling upon others with more expertise. But if you find one with the right combination of skills, one whose demeanor and temperament are compatible with yours, the independent consultant may be the most efficient use of your advertising dollar.

Too often, clients choose agencies based upon who they know: an old friend from school, an acquaintance from church, or a regular tennis partner. Some agencies expect their people to spend a certain amount of time on the golf course or the tennis court wooing new business. They even pay for the club membership. But while your golfing buddy may be a great guy, his agency's ideas about advertising may not mesh with yours.

Friendship and trust are important in your agency relationship. But don't choose your agency solely upon that basis. You may end up paying for it in the end. And friends shouldn't make friends pay for the relationship.

Before selecting your advertising firm or independent consultant, ask to see some of their best work. Look for experience in your industry. While you cannot expect them to be familiar with your specific product or service, look for familiarity with your industry category. For example, you can't necessarily expect them to understand the manufacturing and distribution of semi-circular widgets made of vacuum-molded high-impact titanium plastic. But you would certainly want them to understand the needs of the small manufacturing business.

When shopping around for an agency, don't be fooled by glamour. Some operations are run by hot, ambitious types who are on the make for the big time. They regard your small account really as no account, merely a meal ticket until something better comes along. The work they produce for you is smart-looking, flashy, and generally sells *them*, but rarely you. It lends itself well to full-page, four-color formats, when what you need may be only a quarter page of black and white. Their demeanor is captivating, enthusiastic, and winning. They will go far in this world. Just make sure it's not at your expense.

Better to look for a Total Approach agency. Not one-shot flashy ads. An agency or consultant that develops a series of ads, brochures or collateral pieces around a common theme will likely build a consistent image for you, too. Ultimately, they will help you establish awareness and recognition in your industry, and create a strong association from one marketing effort to the next.

Agencies offer immediate experience and skills you likely don't have. You could probably learn to be a good advertiser through trial and error, but it's easy to waste a lot of money if you don't know what you're doing. An agency assumes the burden of establishing awareness and building your image for you.

Whether you do decide to be your own agency, or whether you simply need to evaluate your agency's work, for better advertising, focus on these four fundamental areas:

Research

Media

Copywriting

Production

Research

The kind of market information that is lying around large companies just waiting to be tapped is often totally absent in small organizations, where executives are long on gut reactions and short on facts. But listening only to yourself can be dangerous. It is important to review your company objectively and impartially. Begin by asking:

- Who buys my product? Then ask,
- Who else *could* buy my product? Could it be used in another way by other customers?
- How is it being distributed?
- What do my customers think about my product?

If you find your customers don't think about your product often enough, you may have an awareness problem. (For more on Research, see Chapter 2.)

Media

Once you know who your customers are, pick the appropriate method of reaching them. This often means choosing and buying media. Media advertising is that artillery barrage before you storm the beaches. It creates awareness and credibility for your firm and builds your image in the minds of your customers. Direct mail works with your advertising. But it often comes out of nowhere, dropped on a desk by a faceless letter carrier. Advertising in the appropriate media can help establish your position in the market and make your company name recognizable when your sales people call, or when you mail out literature. (For more on Media, see Chapter 8.)

The key to good media buying is repetition. If you're buying space in a newspaper or magazine, buy smaller ads and run them more often. Generally, six is the minimum number of times an ad should run in order to create any type of memorable image in the mind of a customer. More is better.

Copywriting

Copywriting is the basis of all advertising. It conveys your message to your customers, presents your company's image to the market, and establishes credibility and awareness for your firm and products. It must be dignified, informative, and noticed. The main objective of any ad or promotional piece is to sell, and subliminally, to convey a message of solidity and reliability. But first, it must capture attention. If it doesn't break the boredom barrier, it's wasted. (For more on Copywriting, see Chapter 6.)

As a handy guide, use the AIDA acronym: Attention, Interest, Description, Action. Grab their attention with a strong headline that includes the main product benefit and, if possible, your company name. Next, create interest in that single product benefit. Describe it in detail. Use examples. Finally, close with a call to action. Ask for the order. Tell your customers how and where to buy your product.

Production

Production value is important. Even the best-written ad will make your company look bad if it isn't produced well. Rule number one: Don't scrimp. Artists take pride in their work as if their creations were their own children. They aim to please themselves. They'll work and rework to achieve a result that meets their personal set of standards. Haggling with them over price will result in off-the-top-of-the-head efforts. Your ads will suffer.

Ideas 5
how to
get them
how to
use them

Good marketing calls for Ideas (with a capital I). But where do they come from? How do you improve your skills in developing them? How can you increase your creative abilities and powers of invention to move your business to a higher (richer) level of success? How do you come by great Ideas?

Try a little applied *imagination*. Contrary to popular opinion, necessity is *not* the mother of invention. Imagination is. Imagination compels us to new ideas, in our business and in our personal lives. Good marketing ideas begin with imagination, too. And you don't need to be a creative genius to come up with compelling ideas. It takes hard work, however, just as does any other task worth doing well.

THE FOUR I'S

You say you can't come up with creative ideas? You're purely a left-brain, analytical type? Hah! Good creative ideas begin with good analysis.

I call the process the "Four I's":

Information

Incubation

Inspiration

Implementation

Information means the gathering of resources. To come up with a good creative marketing idea, immerse yourself in information. All kinds. Trade journals, competitive reports, magazine articles on business trends, even your company's weekly inventory levels.

As an entrepreneur, you likely have most of the necessary information in your head. To prime the pump, review some data that may seem unrelated to your marketing problem. Analyze it. Examine the connections between seemingly unrelated bits of information. Write a few key points. (Our minds retain the written word ten times better than that which is read or spoken.)

Then put it away. Don't think about it for awhile. Allow the information to **Incubate**. Allow your brain to rest. Think about something else entirely. Go to a movie, or tend to your garden. Your brain is chewing on the information you have fed it, analyzing the problem while you do other things. When it is ready, it will provide your conscious mind with an inspiring idea.

Suddenly, the muse strikes: **Inspiration**. It may come while you're driving to work. Or while you're taking a shower. Sometimes it happens in the middle of the night. (It's always a good idea to keep a pad and pencil by your bed for such inspirations. Or better, a micro tape recorder.) Your best ideas will frequently come without warning, when you least expect them. If you don't record them immediately, the odds are strong you'll forget them. Get the ideas down on paper, no matter how crazy they seem at the time.

Sometimes, the idea may be only in the embryo stage. Save it for later. You may come up with the rest of the concept in the future. One client decided to open a discount carpeting outlet, but didn't want to put the word "discount" in his new name. So, we sat and thought and thought and wrote down dozens of ways to visualize "discount." The last one we came up with was a dollar bill torn in half. Today, it's become a well-known symbol among consumers looking for discount carpeting.

The last step, then, is **Implementation**. An idea is no good without it. Many is the brilliant marketing idea that lies dormant and useless simply because it was never implemented. Writing down your inspiration is a first step to implementation. Then, follow-through. Just like your golf swing, your marketing idea won't go as far or end up where you want it without follow-through. Often, this may seem the most daunting of all the steps to creating inspiring promotion ideas. But after you have your idea written down, it's easier to break it into bite-sized chunks and to execute each chunk.

STEAL GOOD MARKETING IDEAS

What happens if you need an idea right now? You don't have time to gather information. No time even for the incubation process. Not to worry. Try resorting to thievery; that is, steal somebody else's good idea. Not in the literal sense, of course. Borrow might be a better term. It's true: There are no new ideas, just new interpretations of old ones.

For starters, steal an idea from this book. That's what it's for. Use the concepts within these pages and adapt them to your product or service. Consider creative ideas that have impressed you in the past. A clever TV commercial, a compelling magazine ad. Think about what you liked about them. Can those ideas be adapted to your product or service?

Next, try thinking about how a big company might solve your marketing problem. How would Procter

& Gamble advertise your product or service? Or McDonald's? As the idea takes shape, adjust it to fit your smaller budget.

Sometimes, thinking about an unrelated business can foster new ideas for yours. You have a friend in another line of work. If you wanted to help her sell more of her product or service, how would you advise her? How can you use that advice in your own business?

"A HALF BUBBLE OFF PLUMB"

Sometimes, "creative" is simply a matter of perspective. Move your imagination "a half bubble off plumb" to find that crazy idea that just might work. When you're stuck for an idea, try looking at your marketing problem from another angle. Ignore conventional logic and use your imagination. Here's a little excercise you can try:

1. Set a problem for yourself.
2. Write down three solutions, totally unrelated.
3. Mix up the solutions till one strikes you as workable.

For instance, let's say your ad won't fit in the space allowed by your trade magazine. Your design is vertical; their space is horizontal. You can redesign the ad, or shorten the copy, or simply eliminate the illustration. Now mix up the solutions: redesign the illustration, eliminate the copy, or shorten the ad.

Or try something completely different. Tip the same ad on its side and change the headline to something like "We'll bend over backward to serve you" or "Our prices will knock you over."

When Avon developed its line of cosmetics and related products, they could have sold them through department stores and competed with Maybelline and Max Factor and a host of others. Did they? No. They ignored traditional channels of distribution and took advantage of the need for self-actualization among the scores of homebound women. Door to door became their means for distribution, and their ticket to success.

Avon used two disparate ideas: the need for part-time employment among women ready to blossom into their professional potential, and the daunting task of supplanting giant competitors in the traditional distribution channel. Together, they formed the basis for Avon's success.

Here's another example: I once was compiling a list of ways to sell cars. On a lark, I wrote down an old retail gimmick: "Buy one, get one free." Taken at face value, the concept could be rather costly for the dealer. But the client loved the idea once we decided simply to offer a model replica of the automobile, painted in the color of the owner's car, with each purchase. "Buy One, Get One Free" made for a compelling advertising headline, and the payoff was an attractive offer. It sold a lot of cars.

Testimonials

It's a mistake to believe that you and your imagination are in a little boat all by yourselves. You aren't. Your customers can have ideas and opinions of their own. In fact, the best ideas often come from your customers. They're called *testimonials*, and they are the foundation of all advertising. Think about it: the satisfied housewife extolling the benefits of Tide laundry detergent, Arnold Palmer and his line of golf equipment, Michael Jordan's shoes, Ed McMahon peddling just about everything. All are examples of testimonials. The customer thinks, "If it's good enough for Michael, it's good enough for me."

But how can you get your customers to talk up your firm? Simple; ask them. If they believe in your product, they may be flattered to endorse it. The easiest (and most credible) testimonials come from your customers. A leading home improvement company ran a contest among its project managers. The manager with the most satisfied customers, evidenced by actual letters, won a trip for two to Hawaii. You can bet every project manager asked his customers for a letter. And the owner was no dummy. All those letters were framed and hung around the showroom. Imagine the impact when browsers came through.

Testimonials from satisfied customers have many uses in your marketing efforts. They add credibility to your company brochure. Enlarged and mounted, they make an effective display at trade shows. Try sending a note to a customer you've been wooing. In your note, mention something another satisfied customer, with whom he's familiar, said about your firm. The uses are as endless as your imagination.

What better way to generate creative ideas than to ask your customers? Let them tell you what they like best about your products. Then let them do your work for you by telling other customers and prospects.

Sort of sounds like something Tom Sawyer would think up to save himself a little work. He'd let Huck Finn do it. Very creative.

Ten 6 commandments of good copywriting

Or Hurry! Learn the Truth About How to Write Miracle Ads

You're on a roll. You've just come up with several brilliant creative ideas and you need them translated into action. You've decided to run a series of newspaper ads (or a few ads in your industry trade journal, or a few radio spots or television spots, or whatever) based upon your dazzling original concepts.

Whether you use a professional writer or do the writing yourself, you want an ad that will stand out among the clutter. A stop-em-dead ad that your customers will read, remember, and act upon.

How do you begin?

Follow the rules. Over time, certain edicts of advertising have evolved. They are the methods of copywriting that garner the greatest response, create the highest awareness levels, and are the most memorable. Yes, there are exceptions to the rules. And some very effective advertisements will occasionally break the rules. But not many.

The First Commandment: Start with a good headline.

Five times as many people read a headline as read the body copy. A good headline is therefore worth 80 cents of your advertising dollar. For that 80 cents, pack in your brand name, product benefit, and a catchy appeal to your target audience.

Don't be afraid of a long headline. Research has shown that headlines of ten words or longer, containing news and information, consistently outperform shorter headlines. Famous ad man David Ogilvy's best headline was "At Sixty Miles Per Hour the Loudest Noise in the New Rolls-Royce Comes from the Electric Clock" (which prompted the chief engineer at Rolls-Royce to comment, "It is time we did something about that damned clock.")

Certain words or phrases work wonders in a headline: how to, suddenly, announcing, miracle, wanted, advice to, the truth about, hurry, compare, and so forth. They may seem like clichés. But they work.

The Second Commandment: Make your copy interesting.

The purpose of the body copy is to convey your sales message in such a way as to make the reader want to read it. The object of your opening statement is to compel the reader to read line two; the purpose of line two is to compel the reader to read line three, and so on. My advice: Write your copy as if you are talking to the person next to you. She has just said, "I want to buy a new gimcrack. Which would you recommend?" Then tell her. Use the language your customers use in everyday conversation. If your customers are electrical engineers, speak in their language. If you're selling to the masses, beware of abstract words or complex sentence structures. Not "eschew obfuscation." Rather, "avoid confusion."

Sometimes, when you need to have a long sentence to explain some complicated thing or another, follow it with a short sentence. Like this. Forget about complete sentences. Remember the way your high school English teacher taught you? With a subject and a predicate? People don't talk that way. You don't need to write your ad copy that way either.

The Third Commandment: Sell the primary benefit, fast.

Look at your product or service. What sets it apart from your competitors'? Why should I want to buy it? How do I benefit by using it? As a consumer, I want to know what's in it for me. I don't care if you've been in business since 1919. Or that your spanking new building has the latest high-tech "state-of-the-art" (oh, please) equipment. What's in it for me?

So tell me, and tell me fast. Research shows readership drops rapidly in the first 50 words of copy, but very little after that. Deliver your primary message and do it quickly. You may not get another chance.

The Fourth Commandment: Sell only one thing.

With rare exception ("Less filling, tastes great," for instance) good ads present one main selling idea, the primary benefit to the consumer. Joy makes your dishes shine. Dawn takes away grease. Ivory is mild to your hands. All three are Procter & Gamble products, yet each offers a different primary benefit. P&G knows that trying to convey more than one idea in an ad confuses customers. So they offer three products with three distinct benefits.

The Fifth Commandment: Use plenty of facts.

The more facts you tell, the more you sell. Research shows an advertisement's success increases as the amount of information increases. The reasoning is simple. Your customer is not a moron; she is your friend. You insult her intelligence if you assume a few adjectives and some simple slogan will convince her to buy your product. She wants to make an informed decision; she wants all the information you can give her. OK, if you're selling chewing gum, I agree there's not a whole lot of facts that are going to sell more gum. But if you're selling hearing aids, ceramic tiles, dry-cleaning services, or drill presses, fill your ads with facts. The more you tell, the more you sell.

You may face a situation in which you and your competitors have similar products with similar characteristics. Rather than promote any minuscule differences as unique product benefits, try using facts to preempt your competition. For example, if your machine performs similarly to others made by your competitors, advertise the safety features that you (and your competitors) employ in its construction. Or the ingredients that you (and your competitors) use that benefit your customers. Your customers will believe those features unique to your product. When advertising master David Ogilvy wrote ad copy for Shell gasoline (a commodity product if ever there was one), he touted the fact that Shell contains "Platformate," an ingredient common to all gasolines. But because they advertised it, Platformate came to be identified as unique to Shell.

Facts are truth. They can be trusted. And so, therefore, can your product. Facts increase reader identification and product credibility. Use them.

The Sixth Commandment: Use testimonials.

They're the next-best thing to word-of-mouth advertising. The endorsement of a fellow consumer is more credible than the witty bromide of an anonymous copywriter. A well-known consumer is even better. And not necessarily expensive.

Say you hear of a celebrity who uses your product. Make an offer of free merchandise in exchange for permission to photograph him or her with your product. The idea of something for nothing appeals to everyone, even celebrities.

The late Burl Ives was a depositor at a California bank that was offering free fishing gear with new account openings. My client offered Mr. Ives some gear he admired for the right to use his photograph in our ads. It was a good deal for both of us. We got a highly respected, recognizable personality endorsing our services. He got some nice fishing gear. Cost: about $100.

The Seventh Commandment: Thou shalt not lie.

Always tell the truth in your advertising and promotion. If you don't, you will be punished. If found out, the government will prosecute you. And consumers will penalize you by not buying your product a second time.

Avoid superlatives. Shun bombast. Truth must be the number-one ethic of your advertising. You can't say your product is the best unless it's been tested against all major competitors and proved reliably superior. Unsubstantiated boasting hurts your credibility. No inflated claims, no lavish promises, no implausible statements. The whole ad falls apart once a shred of disbelief enters the reader's mind.

To say yours is the best, you need to prove it. Some companies go to great lengths to prove their products superior to competitors'. As a brand manager at Procter & Gamble, Roger Smale spent years testing an obscure toothpaste called Crest until he was able to obtain a de facto endorsement from the American Dental Association. He slapped it on the back of every tube ("Crest has been shown to be an effective decay preventive dentifrice when used . . ., etc."). It propelled Crest to its number-one position, and Smale to the presidency of P&G.

Years ago, when I was an executive at the Leo Burnett Advertising Agency, we filmed a television commercial for Glad Garbage and Trash Bags. In the TV spot, an elephant stepped on two bags of garbage, a Glad bag and a generic bag. (The generic bag broke; the Glad bag did not.) Before we could air this spot, we had to prove to the networks that we had used relatively the same garbage in each bag and that the garbage was representative of garbage found in trash cans on the street.

We did. It became known as the "San Francisco Mix." We enlisted the services of a West Coast research firm to determine the size, weight, and contents of the average trash. Somebody actually looked in several hundred San Francisco trash cans, counted the number of bottles, cans, pizza cartons, and banana peels, and concluded that the "average" bag of garbage consisted of:

- 8.3% metal products (cans and lids)
- 12.5% glass
- 3.8% wood
- 12.5% yard waste
- 25.0% food waste
- 36.3% paper products (including at least one pizza box)
- 1.6% plastic

(For the test, we replaced the glass with equal weight of plastic so as not to injure the elephant.)

You probably won't have to go to such lengths to assuage the skepticism of your customers. That doesn't mean you can't be enthusiastic about your product or service. Just don't let your enthusiasm lead you down the path of "hyperbole." Or "hyper" anything. While it's an inherent tendency to believe your product is truly the best, your customers won't unless you can back it up. There's a natural tendency to look sideways at the guy who simply says, "Trust me."

The Eighth Commandment: Ignore awards.

There once was an orator named Aeschines. When he spoke, people said, "My, what a wonderful speech." There was another orator named Demosthenes, ungraceful, with a speech impediment. Yet, when he spoke, people said, "Let us march against Philip!" Aeschines got admiration. Demosthenes got action.

The purpose of advertising is to create action. Not to create notice for the ad itself. Not to win awards.

Action. Advertising must create a desire for the product or service. The desire must be so strong as to compel a person to go out and buy it. Good advertising sells the product without drawing attention to itself.

Some of the biggest and best agencies ignore awards completely. They decline to enter their agency's work in any awards contests. They believe awards create a false emphasis on the ad itself rather than on the product. They also believe awards take time away from the work their best creative people should be doing for their clients.

The Ninth Commandment: Tell them where and when to buy.

Your advertisement has grabbed their attention; they've read your brilliant copy; they're poised to buy. Now what?

Create *action*. If you want them to buy your product, tell them where to find it. If you want to generate leads for your sales force, tell them to call for a free brochure. If you want them to order your product over the telephone, be sure to include your telephone number.

Create *urgency*: "Call today, before we run out of gimcracks at this low, introductory price." Or "Stop in our store today. The sale ends at midnight tonight." Make them act now, before they move on to other things and forget about your great offer.

The Tenth Commandment: Review your ad for three key elements.

First, does it have IMPACT? Does it grab the reader's attention? Does it break the boredom barrier? Most newspapers are about 60-percent advertising; trade journals often contain even more. Will your ad stand out and stop the reader from turning the page?

Second, is it FOCUSED? Does the ad communicate the primary benefit, and *only* that primary benefit, of the product or service being sold? Not 27 other things you wanted to say, like, "We've been at this location for 32 years." (So what.) Or, "And try our gizmo product when you buy our gimcrack, or our new doodads if you don't like gimcracks or gizmos." What are you trying to sell? Remember, only one benefit per ad.

And third, is it HONEST? Would you be willing to show it to your mother?

You might think following these rules would make for pretty dull advertising, that it would cause all ads to look the same, and that remaining within the boundaries outlined here would limit creativity.

Not so. Consider: Shakespeare managed to create many interesting stories while consistently remaining within the limits of iambic pentameter.

Layout 7 and design

There are three basic elements to a good ad:

1. The illustration
   - a drawing or photograph in a print ad
   - the video portion of a television ad
2. The copy
   - in a print ad, the type, including headline, subheads, tag line, logo, etc.
   - the audio portion of a broadcast ad
3. The flow

ILLUSTRATING YOUR AD

A picture is indeed worth a thousand words. That's because we learn a vast majority of what we know with our eyes. Facts presented to the eye and ear are 68 percent better remembered than facts presented to the ear alone. Using photos or drawings in your advertising will make them better read, better remembered. Here are a few hints for making your ads stand out amid the clutter in newspapers and magazines.

Keep it simple

Focus on one thing, one person, or one event. Crowds bewilder your readers.

Show your product

If you sell a product rather than a service, show it in the main illustration. Or show it at the end. But show it somewhere in your ad. Let your reader know what to look for when she goes shopping.

Make your visual match your headline

Your photo or drawing should telegraph the same product benefit you use in your headline.

Use photos

Photos sell better than drawings. And they're better remembered. They're easier for your reader to identify with because they represent reality rather than fantasy. (Exceptions: Drawings work better for humor or when fantasy is the desired effect.)

Use visuals that arouse curiosity

Years ago, Hathaway created mystery by using a model wearing a black eye patch. Their shirts became the number-one brand using an eye patch. More recently, Microsoft uses the intense curiosity of computer users ("Where do you want to go today?") to successfully build their brand image.

Use visuals that demonstrate your product

Master Lock uses a vivid demonstration with a rifle bullet smashing into the product, but the lock doesn't open.

Use visuals that show comparisons

Procter & Gamble's Cheer detergent shows the dramatic difference in the color retention on a colorful shirt after 50 washings in Brand X and after 50 washings in Cheer.

Use visuals to evoke humor

Cartoons work especially well. They have universal appeal and often garner better readership than do photographs. For Nautilus Conditioning Centers, we used a cartoon to poke some lighthearted fun at the intimidating nature of exercise equipment.

LAYING OUT THE COPY

The copy in your print advertisement is an important part of its visual appeal. Good design and layout keep the reader's eye flowing from one element to the next. No clutter. No confusion. No distractions. A good ad layout combines art with motivational psychology. An ad that only looks good is a bad ad. It must also sell.

Here are a few tips for laying out your copy so that your readers' eyes follow your sales pitch from beginning to end.

- Put the headline where your reader will find it first, usually at the top of the page (or right underneath your illustration).

- Your first paragraph should be short, not more than 15 words. Any more and you may scare off your reader.

- If you use long copy (see "The Second Commandment," Chapter 6), use lots of bullet points to break up the paragraphs and increase reader interest.

- For really long copy, insert illustrations now and then.

- Every four or five paragraphs, use a subhead to build interest. Sometimes, a lazy reader will read only your subheads, so use them to deliver the substance of your entire sales pitch.

Pick the part you like

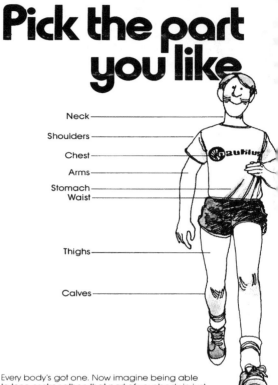

Neck

Shoulders

Chest

Arms

Stomach
Waist

Thighs

Calves

Every body's got one. Now imagine being able to tone or strengthen that part of your body in just 56 seconds, two or three times a week. Studies have shown that long hours of strenuous exercise can do more harm than good. And no matter what form of exercise you use, programs of short, but intensive exercise are best. That's why Nautilus has spent nearly 30 years developing a system for short, but intensive exercise. Designed for men and women on the go. We call it Optimum Fitness in Minimum Time.

Now pick your program.

Almost everybody's program is different, because almost everybody has a different fitness objective, depending on which muscle groups need to be toned or strengthened. With the help of the Nautilus staff, you can design your own program, using just those machines that isolate just those muscle groups that concern you.

Take Martha, for instance.

Magnificent Martha is the Nautilus Leg Extension machine. Not pretty, no. But very effective. If she's part of your program, she'll tone or strengthen the muscles in your thighs in less than a minute. In just as little time, other specially-designed Nautilus machines will tone or strengthen the muscles in other parts of your body.

What makes it work?

The principle of variable muscle resistance. You see, muscles don't have the same strength through their

Full-page newspaper ad for Nautilus of California Conditioning Centers
1. Long headline used initial cap only. 2. Cartoons are often better than photos. 3. Bullet points break up the paragraphs. 4. Columns are often better for long copy. 5. Illustrations ad interest to long copy.

# of your body
he least.

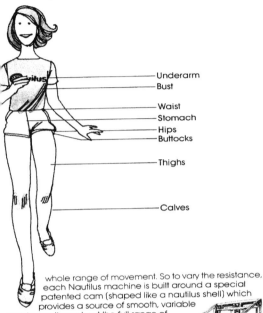

- Underarm
- Bust
- Waist
- Stomach
- Hips
- Buttocks
- Thighs
- Calves

whole range of movement. So to vary the resistance, each Nautilus machine is built around a special patented cam (shaped like a nautilus shell) which provides a source of smooth, variable resistance throughout the full range of muscle movement.

What makes it fun?

Finishing fast. Since most machines do their work in less than a minute, you can complete your whole program in just 20 minutes. Leaving plenty of time to relax in the steamroom. Or in the soothing sauna. Or in the hot, bubbly Jacuzzi.

What more could you ask for?

A free brochure. With all the facts about a Nautilus membership. To get it, just call or write Manager Richard Uphoff. Better yet, stop by and ask him to introduce you to Magnificent Martha, Big Harry, Fabulous Fritz and the other Nautilus machines.

Optimum fitness in minimum time. An investment you make in yourself.

nautilus ic. of California, Inc.
Total Fitness Conditioning Centers
Warner Center Business Park
5940 Variel Avenue • Woodland Hills, California 91367
213/884-1388

- Keep columns narrow, the way newspapers and magazines do.

- Never set your copy in reverse (white type on black background). It's harder to read, and will therefore be ignored.

- Use lower case, like newspapers and magazines. ALL CAPITAL LETTERS ARE MUCH HARDER TO READ.

- If you are using a coupon, put it smack in the middle of your ad to maximize returns.

Most of us grew up reading textbooks, newspapers, and magazines. We became accustomed to the style used by them and find that style easier to read. Emulate them. Use serif type, narrow columns, and uppercase and lowercase letters. Make your ads easy for your customers to read.

BILLBOARDS

A few brief words about billboards: I hate 'em.

Billboards clutter up the highways and ruin what might otherwise be a beautiful bucolic setting along rural routes. Nevertheless, they are ubiquitous, and you may have occasion to use them. So here goes.

All outdoor advertising has one thing in common: Your readers are moving. They can't stop for a second look. A passing driver has just five seconds to read your ad. Five seconds. You have time for just one simple idea. Both the words and pictures must convey your product benefit simply, directly, and fast.

- Be brief.

- Use sans-serif type, as large as possible (the exception to the "emulate-newspapers-and-magazines" rule).

- Use bright colors.
- Use a white background.

Follow these few guidelines and you may not win any classic art awards, but you will produce effective billboards.

How to make the most of media 8

Now that you've honed your copywriting skills and mastered the art of layout and design, you're ready to delve into the mysterious power of media, the buying and selling of time and space. Actually, it's not all that mysterious. But it is powerful.

Consider for a moment what an embarrassment it would be for your salesman to walk into the office of a new prospect and say, "Hi, I'm Joe Dokes," only to have the buyer say, "Joe who?" But consider how much worse it would be to have your salesman try to recover by saying, "You know, Joe Dokes from the Time Tested Tombstone Company," only to meet with, "Time Tested what?"

Your salesman is in trouble. But you're in bigger trouble. Your prospect didn't recognize your company's name because you don't advertise. Sure, you may have sent him a mailing or two. Or even introduced him to your firm at a trade show. But that was last year, or last month, or even last week. If you don't keep your name around constantly, it's forgotten as quickly as last year's Miss America.

Media advertising makes your company name recognizable and remembered. It gives credibility to your products and paves the way for your sales force, or your direct mailings.

Media advertising consists of print (newspapers and magazines), broadcast (radio and television), and the newest form of media: the World Wide Web.

NEWSPAPER ADVERTISING

Newspapers are the most frequently used media for small businesses. They offer a wide variety of cost options, depending on the size of your ad. And they offer a high degree of flexibility, allowing changes up to a few days before the ad is to run. This is a definite advantage when you want quick results. Although magazine ads may seem more glamorous, magazines require long lead times. When you commit to the publication, it may be months before your ad appears in print.

So, let's say you have opted to place an ad in a newspaper. Now you need to ask yourself whether you've found the most suitable setting. In short, will the paper you have selected reach the most prospects customers for the least cost?

A good way to find out which paper works best is to run a little test. Put the same ad with a coupon in several newspapers. Put a different number on the coupons in each newspaper's ad so when the coupons are redeemed, you can count the number of redemptions from each paper and divide by the cost of the ad. You will soon see which newspapers work best for your business.

When testing, don't limit your choice of newspapers to those you read or your spouse reads or the one whose super sales rep is sitting at your desk. The choices are many:

- National newspapers
- Metropolitan newspapers
- Weekly suburban newspapers
- Shoppers classifieds
- Campus newspapers

- Ethnic newspapers
- Alternative/underground newspapers
- Dailies, weeklies, monthlies, etc.

The paper you eventually select will be the one in which you should advertise consistently. It is the one to which you will commit the bulk of your ads, your money, and your hopes. So choose wisely. Make sure it proves itself in the coupon test.

MAGAZINES

Magazines can be an efficient means of targeting your audience. There are magazines covering virtually every market you or I can think of. Magazines for gourmets, chess players, and doll house collectors. Magazines for short people, tall people, even twins.

The beauty of magazines is that they are better suited to lengthy copy than any other medium. That's because people buy magazines in order to spend time with them, unlike newspapers, which are read for the news and discarded. Magazines *engage* their readers. And your magazine ads may do the same.

Print advertisements may be best for explaining a lengthy product message. Charts and diagrams can be used to demonstrate product performance over time. Or to make competitive comparisons. But newspapers and magazines are passive media. Advertising in them assumes the reader has an inherent interest in your product. The readers will frequently pass by an ad if he doesn't know he needs your product.

For that, you need more intrusive media: radio or television.

RADIO ADVERTISING

Radio offers a rich arena for the creative mind.

The ear can be tricked into believing there really is a ship (SFX: fog horn) full of people (SFX: crowd noise) about to crash onto the rocks (SFX: crashing waves) and sink in the shark-infested waters (Music: *Jaws* theme). Unless little Johnny (Boy: "See ya later, Mom") can signal the ship's captain (SFX: fog horn) using his trusty flashlight (Music: build to crescendo) with the Zappum long-life batteries, and save the day (Man: "Thanks, Johnny. You saved us." (Boy: "Don't thank me. Thank my Zappum long-life batteries.") (Music: out).

Radio can be targeted at a specific audience. Each radio station appeals to a very select group of listeners. And ratings companies monitor exactly who is listening when. So you can pick your station based on how closely it matches your target customers.

But radio has its limitations, too. Most people don't "listen" to radio; they simply "hear" it. It serves as background noise while they work, or while they drive. So unless your radio spot is unique and can grab the "hearers" and make them "listeners," use radio cautiously.

TELEVISION ADVERTISING

The most intrusive medium is television. You watch a program and suddenly the program is interrupted by a commercial. So, you watch it, too. Oh, sure. There are "zappers" out there who have discovered the power of the remote control, who have learned to "zap" past commercials, switching channels, holding the plots of three American Movie Classics in their heads at the same time. Or trying not to miss one precious moment of the clown juggling cigar boxes on channel 61. But the fact remains, TV intrudes on our lives every moment it is turned on. It offers the best opportunity to create awareness for your product or service in the minds of your customers.

The cost of television advertising is not for the weakhearted. For example, the average cost of producing a 30-second television spot today is $70,000. Gulp. Take a deep breath. You're probably thinking, "I can't afford a 1-second spot, let alone a 30-second spot." But that price tag is deceiving. That $70,000 average includes all those high-priced beer and soft drink commercials featuring multiple scenes (each one must be directed and shot individually), shot on location (travel and lodging are extra), with a cast of many (each model must be paid; celebrities often receive huge amounts).

Your TV spot can be much more basic and less costly. A simple message with no on-camera actors can often be produced for a few thousand dollars. Effectively written, your TV ad can be beneficial to your marketing efforts.

If you decide to use this powerful medium to carry your message, here are three simple guidelines to help you maximize your effectiveness and avoid wasting a lot of money.

What you show is more important than what you say

Television is a visual medium. Research has shown that if you say something that you don't also illustrate, the viewer immediately forgets it. Make your pictures tell the story; the only purpose of the words is to reinforce what is shown. In short, if you aren't going to show it, don't say it. Here's a useful test: Try turning off the sound on your TV spot. If it doesn't sell without the sound, you're in trouble.

Don't try to do too much with your 30 seconds

Use only 75 words or less. More than that makes it hard to comprehend your message. Make only one (or at most, two) selling points: ("Schmooz is gentle to your hands. And now it's available at Dokes Department stores.") Too many selling points in one ad confuse the viewer.

Use your product's name at least three times in the 30 seconds

The average consumer sees more than 1,000 commercials a month. If you want her to remember your product, show her both the product (in the package you want her to look for) and the product benefit. Repeat your major selling promise at least twice; illustrate it visually; show it as a super or subtitle on the screen. Remember, your primary objective is not to entertain. It is to make sure your viewer remembers your product next time she decides to make a purchase.

One other point: If you plan on using television as a part of your marketing mix, retain a media buying service. They usually charge about 6 percent of the cost of your media purchase, but they'll save you a lot more than 6 percent. You may think you can negotiate a good deal with the local TV station, but media buying services buy millions of dollars in media every month and have far more buying power than your small business.

CABLE TELEVISION

Cable TV is usually more affordable than network television. The numerous shows on cable today, like magazines, make cable an efficient means of targeting your audience. You can pinpoint your target market by buying ads on only those shows that appeal to them. Cable eliminates a lot of waste.

For instance, let's say you sell lumber and building supplies. You could buy expensive spots on network TV shows, such as sports and movies, that appeal to your target. Or you could buy far less expensive cable spots on Bob Vila's cable show, "Home Again," "HouseSmart! with Lynnette Jennings" or some other home repair shows. If you need television to tell your product's story, cable is often the most efficient use of your limited marketing budget.

REACH VS. FREQUENCY

All media works on the basis of "reach" and "frequency." Reach is the number of new people that sees (or hears) your advertisement. Frequency is the number of times they see it. Reach is measured in Gross Rating Points (GRPs). One gross rating point is 1 percent of the viewing (or listening, in the case of radio) public. If there are 100,000 TV sets in your city, one GRP is 1,000 TVs.

A good rule of thumb: To create an impression among TV viewers, you need to deliver a minimum of 150 GRPs per month for *at least three months*. To introduce a *new* product, figure 500 GRPs a month for at least the first three months and 150 GRPs per month for the three months after that.

Reach creates awareness. Frequency sells. The subliminal effect of seeing an advertisement repeatedly creates credibility, connecting that company to that class of product in the customer's mind. So, just because you're tired of seeing the same ads for your products doesn't mean your customers are. They haven't seen them as often as you have. Don't be afraid to run your ads over and over again. And then, when you're so tired of them you could scream, run them again.

Target Rating Points While Gross Rating Points (GRPs) are a percent of the total viewing audience, Target Rating Points (TRPs) are a percent of your target audience. If your product is bought only by women, your TRPs are measured as a percent of women watching your commercial. Always use TRPs when judging the efficiency of your media.

It took millions to develop the association between "Kleenex" and tissues, "Xerox" and copies. But that sort of status can be achieved by your business through constant repetition. Repetition is important throughout all your marketing efforts. Use the same theme, tag line, even the same words if possible in your TV advertising, your print ads, mailings, at trade shows, perhaps even on your company letterhead.

Repetition helps your prospects remember. If you place a big ad in a newspaper or magazine, get reprints. Mail them to all your customers and potential customers. Enlarge them and display them in your booth at trade shows. Hang them up in your place of business. Feature them in your direct mailings.

Repeat your media message in your direct mailings. By itself, your brochure or company literature may lack the impact of media advertising. But when it features an ad that your customers have seen in the media, it further enhances your company's credibility and adds to that all-important frequency. The more often your customers see your ads, the better the ads sell.

The media advertising creates awareness, builds your image in the minds of your customers. It establishes your position in the market. So when your direct mailing hits their desk, they recognize your name, read your mailing, and respond. And when your salesman calls on a new prospect, the prospect may not know his name, but he'll know yours.

FLIGHTING AND FRONT LOADING

You can stretch your media budget by "flighting." Flighting means staggering your use of media. For example, let's say you can afford 50 GRPs a week for 12 weeks (a total of 600 GRPs). Rather than run 50 GRPs each week, consider running 100 every other week. You'll achieve more impact by creating the illusion you're around all the time. Viewers won't know you're not on the air during the off week.

They'll simply assume they just weren't watching when your ads were running.

Here is how flighting looks in graph form.

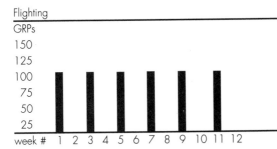

Another effective media buying maneuver is called "front loading," that is, heavily saturating your audience with your message in the first few weeks of your campaign and then tapering off. For example, try running 100 GRPs during the first few weeks and 25 during each of the next eight weeks. Here is how front loading looks on a graph.

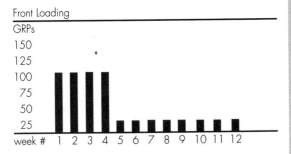

A combination of flighting and front loading is shown in the following example:

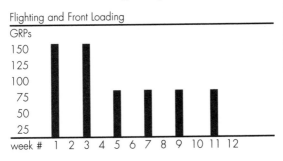

MULTIPLE IMPRESSIONS

By combining a variety of media—newspaper ads, radio spots, direct mailings—you can increase awareness of all your advertising and maximize your efforts. If a prospect hears your ad on the radio, reads your advertisement in the newspaper, and sees your ad in a trade magazine, he'll be more apt to read your brochure when it lands on his desk. He'll also be more apt to call you over a competitor when it's time to buy.

The more often your customers see your ads, and the more diversified their exposure to your name and product benefit, the more apt they are to purchase. Large companies simultaneously run TV spots, newspaper ads, and radio spots, mail brochures, dealer letters, and product announcements, and get wide coverage for their products in trade magazines and local newspapers.

So if you're contemplating an ad campaign, make it work harder for you by spreading it across several media.

THE WORLD WIDE WEB

Business Week calls it "The most important invention since Velcro." But it's bigger than that. It's bigger than Saran Wrap. Bigger than Band-Aids. More important even than Madonna. It's the World Wide Web. And it's the way the world will communicate in the next century.

Think of it. Your computer will be your communications center. Your telephone, your CD player, your mailbox (e-mail), filing cabinet, library, even your favorite TV show. Everything available on your computer screen. All coming to you through cyberspace.

Businesses have been quick to recognize the web's potential. It's the ability to "talk" on the Internet with friends, family, and, most important, *customers* that has given the World Wide Web its explosive growth. The sheer excitement of real-time interaction with prospects and customers is causing a rush to the Web unseen since the days of the Klondike.

The Web is a whole new communications medium. A new way to reach your customers. Imagine for a moment that your firm's product or service is water. Television, then, is like a hose spraying a crowd, and you hope some will enjoy getting wet. Direct mail is like a squirt gun aimed only at those who you think want to get wet. Marketing on the Web is like a pond. Prospects can visit, dive in as deep as they want, swim as long as they like. Your Web site isn't something people read; it is something they do.

It's no wonder companies such as Miller Brewing (http://www.mgdtaproom.com), McDonald's (http://www.mcdonalds.com), Motorola (http://www.motorola.com), even Sleepy Eye Lake Vacation Hideaway (http://www.execpc.com/~maryk) are rushing to the Web. Worldwide, there are more than five million companies with Web sites. By the year 2000, there will be more than a billion people using the Web, an increase of nearly 8 percent *every* month.

Like a trade show, the web may not get your company lots of leads or bring you a slew of sales. But you are conspicuous by your absence.

> *"No Web site, huh?"*
>
> *"Can't I get your latest catalog off the Web?"*
>
> *"I've already downloaded your competitor's product information."*

If you can't be shamed into becoming "Web literate," here are ten reasons that may appeal to your sense of logic.

1. Increase your visibility
2. Improve service for your current customers
3. Give a leading-edge corporate image
4. Decrease your communications costs
5. Develop online customers

6. Distribute information around the globe
7. Update product information instantly
8. Expand your market
9. Real-time communications
10. Your competitor is there

Somewhere in your firm there is information that is valuable to people trying to buy products you sell. The Web lets you *offer* that information to the world with unprecedented speed and flexibility. Update price changes daily. Update product data sheets instantly. Send blueprints and product spec sheets. Add new products to your catalog. Delete old ones.

If that isn't enough to lure you in for a closer look, the Web also has multimedia capabilities. Text, graphics, video, and sound. Users can read about your product, see a photograph of it in various colors, hear you talk about it. They can even watch video clips of your product in action.

Cyberspace is a New Age marketing medium that offers more than Olde World options. So it requires new thinking, new strategies, and a new approach. When you have only 30 seconds to deliver your message on TV or radio or you can afford to run only a quarter-page ad in the newspaper or magazine, some information must be sacrificed. Brochures and catalogs can present longer messages, but these, too, have limitations of space and cost. What's more, none of these marketing tactics offer your prospect a chance to interact with your company.

Your Web site does. Prospective customers tap into your organization and take the information they want, when they want it. They educate themselves. Your Web site provides instant delivery of promotional materials to a worldwide list of self-selected prospects at a fraction of the cost of a sales call.

While your Web site can never replace the face-to-face benefits of personal selling, it can serve as a supplement to your sales force, reaching new customers, expanding your sales potential, making your company's products available around the world. Think of the man-hours you can save in sales training, travel time, and supervision. Never sit in your prospect's waiting room again. Never be caught without the latest catalog or price list. It's all on your Web site.

The best Web site is simple and straightforward. Design is crucial. Just as your sales staff is the face of your company, your Web site has only one chance to make a first impression. Your Web site is the prospect's electronic visit to your company. Think: IMAGE. What does the place look like? Is there someone there to greet them in a courteous and professional manner? Are they treated as though they are welcome? Your Web site requires the same care in copywriting, graphic design, and attention to detail as your best advertising piece, product catalog, or trade show exhibit.

Start by making your home page (the first page of your Web site, the first one a user will see) easy to view, even for the slowest connectors. All you really need is your corporate logo, your mission statement, and a few small graphic icons that link the user to various sites. One link could send a prospective customer to your product catalog; another might offer service and support; still another might allow users to send e-mail back to your company.

Once a user has found your catalog, he can download information on specific products. You may even provide an order form for selling right off your Web page. Visitors can request that a brochure or other literature be mailed to them by filling in a form with their name, company, address, and phone number. You can add these to your mailing list.

Keep your whole Web site friendly, functional, and fun. Friendly, because it has to be easy to use, even for computer novices with the slowest equipment. Functional, so there is a clear benefit to users when they get there.

And fun, because that's what the World Wide Web is all about.

Using publicity to stretch your marketing budget

9

Here's how to use publicity when you need your name in the paper but you don't want to pay for it.

As we saw in the prior chapter, media can be expensive. Publicity, on the other hand, can be cost-free. It also has another advantage. Because it is presented in the press as a story, it has more credibility with readers than paid advertising.

Remember the old Hollywood adage: It doesn't matter what they say about you so long as they spell your name right? Well, that may be great for movie stars, but your company needs *positive* publicity. Here are a few hints to help your firm maximize its marketing dollar and build a positive public image.

Editors and columnists depend upon industry to keep them informed of changing technology and the latest innovations. You can provide a vital service by submitting that information in the form of a press release. Don't be afraid to attempt it yourself, but try to make life easy for your editor. Summarize the important points with a headline. Put all the salient points (who, what, where, why, when) up front, in the first paragraph. The less the editor has to edit, the greater the chance she will use your material.

Always put "For Immediate Release" or "For Release" (and the date the story will be current) at the top of the first page. Be sure to include your name and telephone number at the beginning of the release. The editor may want to check certain details for accuracy. Or she may want to expand on your story.

According to research, a story with a picture is read about eight times more often than one without. So, send along a black-and-white photograph (5" x 7" is best) with the press release. Hint: When quoting a person mentioned by name, always include the person's age.

Because the editor "depends" upon that news, it must be accurate. And it must not smack of advertising. Leave out your company's advertising adjectives or endorsements. Skip the superlatives; they won't print them anyway, and they can prejudice an editor against you. The editor knows your press release has been prepared to benefit your company, but it also must benefit her readers.

WHAT SHOULD BE PUBLICIZED?

If you have something of interest happening at your company, send your industry trade journals a press release.

The new product

Most trade journals have a new products/services section. It provides information that may be important to the readers. If you have a new machine that vastly improves the quality or delivery time of your products, you actually provide a vital service by submitting that information to your trade journal editors so they in turn can publish it for their readers.

The grand opening

The new addition or remodeling also makes for good publicity. Any time you expand quarters, send out a press release. Mention the greater convenience, additional elbow room, how it will benefit the readers of the article, your potential customers.

The new employee

Adding a new person warrants a press release. A new executive's first responsibility should be to submit a brief autobiography and picture (good items to have in the employee files anyway). They can serve as the basis for a press release. The release should include who she is, what she will be doing, what she is expected to accomplish (here's where you slip in the commercial about specific areas of expertise), and details about her education, experience, associations, and family. Some publications have special sections for new faces. They are usually widely read.

The new customer

When you sign a big new account, send a press release (with the account's permission, of course). Let everyone know. It's one more opportunity to put your name before the public. It also gives you credibility in your industry. People in related businesses will think that you must be experts in that field, or else Harry at XYZ Company wouldn't be buying from you.

When nothing else is happening, make news

The industry "prediction" is always good. For example, "Joe Dokes, President of Okey Doke Computer Supplies, predicts the fax machine will go the way of the dodo bird by the year 2000. 'The world will communicate via e-mail,' said Dokes. 'The Internet is the wave of the future. It's faster, cheaper, and more accurate . . .,' etc. etc."

The secret of this technique is to make a statement that is intriguing, maybe even fantastic, but never unbelieveable. You endow the quoted person with instant expertise. He has made a publicized prediction; he must therefore be a revered seer. Everyone wants to work with a company headed by such a renowned and respected sage.

Another device you can use to break into the media is a statement about the condition of the economy: It's good, but it could get worse; it's bad, but it will get better. Back it up with a few accurate statistics and the implications for your industry, and you have yourself an interesting news release.

CHOOSING A PUBLIC RELATIONS AGENCY

There is a great deal of publicity your company can generate on its own. The time may come when you need expert advice, however. You may have a problem at your company that needs delicate handling in the press. Or you may have a need for a major article or series of articles on your company to bolster your prestige in the industry.

A publicist or public relations specialist may be necessary. If so, choose one small enough to pay your company the attention it requires. Avoid the revolving-door agencies, long on promises but short on delivery, in which accounts come and go. Usually, they send in their big guns to secure the account, then turn you over to an itinerant junior looking to build his résumé, or worse, a rank neophyte.

For your small business, your best bet is a small shop in which the principals will give you their expertise because your account is important. Your publicist should have well-developed relations with the press and a track record of achievement in your specific area of need. A good publicist should know many editors on a first-name basis.

One good way to choose a public relations firm is to call a few local journalists, editors, or columnists.

Tell them about your company and its publicity needs. Ask them whom they respect, who they like to work with.

Newspapers and magazines receive hundreds, sometimes thousands of submissions every day. Some editors have piles of submissions several feet high awaiting their perusal. And only 40 percent of the average daily newspaper is editorial. The rest is advertising. So the competition for space is intense. A good publicist should be able to get your story on top of the pile.

Remember, publicity gives you less control than advertising. There is no guarantee when or even if your article will run. Your publicist may work for weeks, even months, preparing a piece and putting it before the proper magazine and newspaper editors. But reasons beyond your publicist's control may prevent your story from appearing within the time frame you desire.

Be patient. It's worth the wait. Because of its credibility, editorial publicity is generally considered to be worth more than ten times the same amount of space in paid advertising. And it's an effective way to stretch your marketing budget.

Be a Good Neighbor

Donate your product or service to a worthy cause. Neighborly? Yes, but it's also good business. The charity may mention your company in its literature. And, with a little savvy public relations, you may create an image associating your firm with worthy endeavors.

A client of mine owns a local dry cleaning chain. He faced a new competitor across the street from one of his stores. As part of our marketing efforts to check this threat, we created a scholarship fund at the local high school, a $500.00 good citizenship award. It serves as a reminder to the community that my client has been their neighborhood dry cleaner for many years. It also creates awareness of the firm among high school students, a prime source of employees for this service business.

Consider donating products or services to your local public television station. You gain visibility among viewers (there are many avid TV Auction watchers), and you may pick up new customers from those who sample your product.

Review the charitable organizations in your community that attract people who fit your target-customer profile. If they notice your firm donating time or services, they may become your customers. Best of all, you champion an admirable crusade. And you may get to know some nice people.

Introducing a new product

Every company needs new products in order to grow. Both industrial customers and consumers expect a stream of new and improved products to suit their changing needs and wants.

Your competitors are certainly doing their best to meet these expectations. In a sense, it becomes increasingly risky NOT to introduce new products.

At the same time, innovation can be risky business. Think about Ford's ill-fated Edsel, DuPont's Corfam (synthetic leather), or Xerox's venture into computers. The French Concorde aircraft will probably never recover its investment. Statistics indicate more than 10,000 new products are introduced every year. A majority fail in the first year; more than 80 percent in the first three.

The introductory period of the product is extremely important. It sets the pace for future product growth, and it creates the impression among your customers and prospects that your company is innovative and creative. But if not executed properly, it may break the back of your company's profit picture.

Even if your new product is a huge success, your competitors may be quick to imitate it. Some new products are copied by rivals so quickly that the race to be first on the market may take on grotesque proportions. Years ago, the folks at Alberto-Culver got wind of a new shampoo being tested by Procter & Gamble. They were so eager to beat P & G to the market with their own version that they developed a product name and filmed TV commercials before they had even finished developing the product.

You face a dilemma: You need to develop new products, yet the odds against success are hefty.

Introducing a new product or service to your customers requires planning, perseverance, and guts. Here are three *Naked Marketing* ideas to keep in mind to help you improve your odds of success:

1. The right product
2. The right timing
3. The right people

THE RIGHT PRODUCT

It's true you only get one chance to make a first impression. Don't blow it. Make sure your new product or service is the best it can be before you foist it on an unsuspecting public. Your customers' attitudes the first time they see or try your product will stay with them a long time.

A client, who shall remain nameless, ordered up some impactful advertisements and a heavy media schedule for a new cleaning product that had been rushed through the research and development process without sufficient testing.

The ads worked. The product flew off the shelves. And flew right back to the stores a week later for refunds. The product had separated into a gooey mess, disgusting to look at and totally ineffective as a cleaner. A minor adjustment in the mixing process solved the problem, but by then it was too late. Our credibility was lost. Customers never bought the product again even after we fixed it. The retailers were angry, too. They were stuck processing all the refunds.

Proper research and testing in the prototype stage of development will pay dividends in the long run. Three key steps:

1. The product must satisfy a consumer need
2. The product must perform up to or in excess of expectations under normal use and conditions
3. The product can be produced and sold at a profit

No matter how well you conceive and execute a marketing strategy, if your product isn't perfect, it'll die. The better your marketing plan, the faster its demise. The sooner your customers hear about and try your product, the sooner they discover whether it meets their needs. If it doesn't, your terrific marketing plan will cause your lousy new product to fail that much sooner. Nothing will destroy a bad product faster than good marketing.

THE RIGHT TIMING

Timing is important, too. Any number of external factors may delay your introduction. If your new product is replacing an old one, you may wish to hold up shipments until the old product's stock is depleted. It may make sense to defer distribution until after the big industry trade show. Or if your product is seasonal, you may wish to hold off until the start of the selling season.

When the external timing is right, make sure all the internal pieces are in place before launching your new product. That means your new product is ready for market (see The Right Product). It also means your sales people are ready, your distribution system is ready, and your marketing program is ready.

Several years ago, a client offered an attractive gym bag free with the purchase of a new, but inexpensive piece of exercise equipment. The bags were to contain literature promoting other, more expensive equipment. We bought heavy advertising schedules well in advance and ordered lots of gym bags. But by the start of the event, a SNAFU at the printer left us with no sales literature for the first two weeks of the 30-day promotion.

The attractive offer sold lots of the new, low-margin equipment. Unfortunately, the company lost a bundle on the bags and couldn't make it up on sales of the higher profit equipment because of the missing literature.

THE RIGHT PEOPLE

Out there, among the buying public, are people who buy stuff simply because it's new. They're called *early adopters* and they are fascinated by anything their friends and neighbors haven't heard of yet. They buy the latest shampoo, the hottest new car, the intriguing new gizmo with the cutting-edge techno doodad.

Smart marketers love them. These pioneers are the first wave of consumers for new products. They can tell you whether your introduction will generate enough repeat purchasers to make it in this competitive world.

On the other side of the spectrum, you have the *late adopters*. These cautious consumers don't cotton to strangers and don't trust anything they haven't heard of. They won't try your new product simply because it *IS* a new product.

Then there are those folks smack dab in the middle. They represent about 80 percent of your target market. They want to buy your product, but before they do, they have to be convinced it's better than what they have now. They are willing to listen to your sales pitch if it's interesting. But, it had better be persuasive. It had better tell them *why* your product is good, not just that it is new.

Target your sales pitch to this 80 percent. Skip the early adopters; they'll buy your product anyhow simply because it's new. And skip the late adopters, too. They may come around in time, once your product is established. Aim squarely at that middle majority. And give them solid reasons to buy your product.

First, tell them why *new* is better. In your marketing materials, use words such as new, introducing, hurry, how to, and announcing (see Chapter 6). Express enthusiasm, a spirit of excitement in all your marketing efforts. Show your confidence in the new product or service. Enthusiasm is contagious; your customers will share your excitement if your reasons clearly define why your new product is better.

Then, run big ads. Lots of them. Remember, no one has heard of your new product. Coordinate multiple media efforts—radio, newspapers, publicity, brochures, telemarketing, the works. Plan on spending a big chunk of your marketing budget now, during the introductory period. Inundate your target market with your message. Subsequent advertising will be more effective if you have created sufficient awareness among your prospects.

Legally, you have six months to claim your product is new. After that, be ready with phase two of your new product introduction. In this phase, your marketing efforts should point out *how well accepted* the product is. Use testimonials from your pioneer users, those early adopters. Show how others just like those in your target market are already benefiting from your new product. Maintain the momentum of your introduction for as long as possible.

The introductory period is a critical time in the success of your new product or service. If your product is right, the timing is right, and you market it to the right people, you greatly reduce your risk of failure.

11
Selling

Sales are food. Selling is what you do to feed your company. To acquire your food, you can either hunt or you can farm. One is far easier, and cheaper, than the other.

HUNTING VS. FARMING

To *hunt* is to seek new customers, to acquire them in one of two ways: selling more product to new customers in your market or finding new uses for the same product in a different market.

Either way is expensive. To sell more product to new users in your market, you can try to convince nonusers (folks who don't use your type of product) that they need to use your product. Or you can spend lots of money on advertising and promotion to convince users of a competitive product to abandon the competitor and buy your product instead. Marketers call this buying market share. Prepare to spend big bucks. Why? Consumers have inertia. They are often reluctant to change their buying patterns unless firmly convinced of the benefits of a competing product. It may take unhealthy amounts of time, money, and patience to persuade them to buy yours.

Another method of hunting new customers is to find new uses for your product in a different market. This can be even costlier.

For example, suppose your company makes gooseneck lamps for home and office. You notice that they also work well as a reading light on the piano. A virgin market. All sorts of opportunities for new sales. But hold on. You will need to create awareness in this new market. After all, nobody's heard of you. You'll need an advertising and promotion program geared to the piano market, with brochures, catalogs, and a sales staff to call on all your new customers.

In short, hunting is costly. It means changing people's daily habits and customs.

You do, however, have another option: reinforce existing habits and customs. It's called farming. To *farm* is to grow more sales from your existing customers. Much easier. Much cheaper. Statistics show that the cost of selling to new customers is more than 12 times as expensive as selling to current customers. Think about it. Twelve times more expensive.

When you farm, you don't need to create awareness and credibility with your customers. They already know you and trust you. Cultivate them. Sell more of your products or services to them.

There are many different types of farming. One common one I call rotation farming, in which the customer comes back periodically for regularly scheduled appointments.

For instance, a woman who owns a hair salon has many customers who stop in only when it's convenient. What happens when they find her shop busy and can't be fit into her schedule? If it happens too often, they begin going elsewhere. I suggested she review her appointment book and call every customer about four or five weeks after the last appointment to schedule a new one. She did, and business increased more than 20 percent.

The same works for any business. If you operate a garage, schedule periodic oil changes with your regular customers. They'll appreciate the reminder, and your business will increase.

Florists can use rotation farming. One client contacted his best customers and asked them for their wedding anniversaries and spouse's birthday. He keeps the dates on file in his database and reviews them periodically. Then, shortly before each date, he calls them and suggests a floral arrangement for the occasion.

Here are a few other farming ideas to help increase your yield.

SUGGESTIVE SELLING

Ever notice when you go into a fast-food restaurant, they always ask if you want fries with your order? Likewise, when you buy shoes, the sales person asks if you would also like polish or shoe trees? That's suggestive selling. It's the easiest way to build sales. Your customer is already in a buying mood. You are simply suggesting she spend a little extra to enhance the quality of her purchase.

Suggestive selling aims to trigger an additional purchase. In other words, if you have already sold 'em one thing, they trust you enough to buy from you already, so sell 'em something else at the same time, while they are in a buying mood.

Make suggestive selling an integral part of your sales philosophy. Reward your sales force for add-on sales. Offer bonus commissions or prizes for reaching accessory sales goals. Try mixing and matching products in your catalog. Show how different parts work together: the shoes and hat that go with the dress, the drill bits that work best in the new press, or the special oil that makes that drill press operate more efficiently.

Your customers are happy to have received this extra advice. They now know what makes the item they have just bought work best. You're happy because you have maximized your sales with the least amount of cost.

Sell accessories

If you sell her a desk, suggest a matching chair or lamp. If he buys your accounting services, suggest financial-planning options as well. If they want a microwave, sell them a cookbook and a service warranty, too.

A company I once owned manufactured uniforms for schools of nursing. It was a tough business, with cheap offshore competitors and minimal profit margins. Where we made our biggest return was selling those same students sweaters, stethoscopes, sphygmomanometers (blood pressure kits), and watches with glow-in-the-dark numerals and sweep second hands. We paid the bills with uniforms, but we made our profit from accessories.

Trade up

Last year, Larry bought a standard doodad from you. This year, sell him the deluxe model. Once Larry becomes acquainted with your product or service, it's easier to sell him on the benefits of the same product with expanded capabilities, a few more bells, a couple of whistles, and a maintenance agreement. Every year, your industry changes, innovations occur, equipment becomes outdated. Keep your current customers informed of your company's marvelous new innovations they shouldn't be without. Then, trade them up next year.

Incentive selling

It works. Free gifts, premiums, and discounts all serve as effective means of building more sales from your existing customer base. Try offering a free gift with any purchase over a given amount. Large retailers of electronics and appliances use this method effectively. Imagine, some huckster in a loud plaid jacket is screaming "Get a bike, get a bike, get a bike! That's right!" (Hucksters always scream in exclamation points!) "Come on down to Ajax Appliances and get a free ten-speed bicycle with any major appliance!" It's amazing how many of those no-name brand bikes you see pedaling along on a Sunday afternoon.

Distinctive Coca-Cola glasses never fail to attract buyers at fast-food restaurants. Paying an extra 50 cents (cost to restaurant, about 21 cents each) for a collector glass you can take home seems a real bargain. Think about how your business could package its product with a sure winner to increase your sales.

Special discounts

Offer special discounts for larger purchases. I once saw a farmer selling eggs by the side of the road. Her sign said, "10% off any purchase of 13 or more." After inquiring, I discovered she sold her eggs only by the dozen. The promotion was a sham, but I bought two dozen anyway just because I liked her sense of humor and her marketing moxie.

Complete systems

This is the age of convenience. People want an easy "turnkey" operation because of its convenience. If your customer wants to build a new plant, he can make all the separate decisions himself, hire architects, engineers, contractors, legal staff, and so on. Or he can call you because you offer all these services in one complete package. Even if it's beyond your expertise, farm out the related services, but offer the complete package.

GE Medical Systems, for instance, sells not just a piece of high-tech health care hardware, but a whole set of accompanying services, including instruction, canned software programs, programming services, financing, delivery arrangements, and maintenance and repair programs. Savvy companies recognize that this holistic approach is a great way to grow more business.

The last word

To hunt, or to farm. Your company needs both. Hunting replaces those customers who decide to change suppliers, go out of business, or move away. So you will always need to hunt. But farming is still easier, cheaper, and more effective for growing your sales and profitability.

Whether hunting or farming, it's up to your people to make your sales quotas. Your employees answer the telephone and take a customer's order. They venture out to call on customers. Or they take the cash at the cash register.

THAT ALL-IMPORTANT SALES FORCE

How do you maximize the effectiveness of your sales staff? How do you get them passionate about your products? What great elixir can you feed them to get them to charge out on cold mornings and break their backs for you? The obvious answer, of course, is money. It seems to be what motivates most of them to sell and to excel.

But your sales staff also needs love. They spend their days amid rejection and complaints, courting the favor of petulant purchasing agents and belligerent buyers. They are often away from the comforts of house and laundry for long periods of time. Along with the commission check, they need the ego gratification of corporate recognition, a symbolic pat on the back for a job well done. And that recognition should be visible to their peers.

A sales meeting is an opportunity to publicly acknowledge your sales people's importance. They need to know that, while they're out there doing battle with the hostiles, somebody back home really does care about what they think, feel, and need. Sales meetings furnish the sales people with a feeling of belonging, of being a part of the team. And the fact is, they're good business.

Once a year, plan a big bash (banquet, golf outing, or field trip to a supplier, for example) with awards and some form of entertainment. If you have lots of extra money floating around (which most small companies don't), hold your sales meeting in some exotic locale. Spend a week at a tropical resort. Or charter a boat. But for a small company on a budget, the two most practical ways of holding a sales meeting are to bring everybody to your company's hometown or meet at the annual trade convention.

The sales meeting at your company has several advantages: Your home staff gets a chance to meet and greet the folks in the field. And the folks in the field get a chance to tour the factory, see the products being assembled, talk to the production department about delivery schedules, review office procedures, and build coalitions with the various department heads one-on-one. Sales people in the field tend to think only of their customers and their commissions. But given a clearer understanding of the headquarters systems and challenges, they develop an appreciation for why orders cannot always be shipped when and how they want them.

Meeting at the annual trade show saves money. Most sales people have to attend the show anyway, so why not get them all together there for your own annual meeting? Trade shows offer opportunities for guest speakers, industry experts already in attendance that could add insight to your meeting. Consider inviting one or two suppliers or industry gurus to address your sales staff. While most will be happy to oblige without compensation, be sure to reward them for their time with a token gift, nicely packaged.

Speaking of gifts, it's also a good idea to leave some with your sales force. Some token of appreciation, even a T-shirt or corporate coffee mug, reminds them that they're loved. These tokens, however, are not a substitute for annual or quarterly sales awards. These should be significant items, earnest expressions of corporate appreciation for a job well done.

Every sales meeting should have a planned agenda. Start the meeting with a brief (that's BRIEF) speech by the president ("Hi glad to see you all here we've had a great year and let's all look forward to a great future now here's Joe.") followed by the sales manager.

The sales manager is like the coach of a football or basketball team. Part teacher, part cheerleader, part confessor. Mostly motivator. His speech should be upbeat, inspiring, action-packed, and full of promise for a bright future. If the past year has indeed been a poor one, however, face up to it honestly, explain how the problems are being addressed, and that you can all look forward to a bright, action-packed future full of promise.

Pace, pace, pace. Don't give anyone time to develop that glassy-eyed stare so common among aggressive type-A sales people bored with a program. Keep the meeting moving.

Agenda topics should include new products or services now being offered by the company, production problems and delivery schedules, and new advertising or other sales support. Allow time for "new business." Let your sales people tell you what their customers are asking for. After all, they're the ones who see them every day.

Your sales staff can be a tremendous source of ideas for new products and services, suggesting better ways to serve your clients. And better ways for them to fill their sales quotas. A sharp sales woman at a client of mine noticed that the three-ring binders she was selling to office-supply centers were also being bought by a local photo studio. She investigated and discovered the photo studio was selling the binders as photo albums. We promptly dummied up some literature aimed at the photo-supply business and, suddenly, a whole new market was born.

Invite outside speakers to your meeting. Your product manager, a vendor, a money manager, or even an English teacher to help polish sales letters and presentations. Your sales people can benefit from their expertise. And it shows that you acknowledge your staff's importance. Most important, it tells them somebody back home really does care about what they think, feel, and need. It tells them they're loved.

Sometimes, it's not always possible to call on every customer personally. Some hunting and farming may need to be conducted by mail, or fax, or via e-mail over the World Wide Web. If so, you need to communicate your selling proposition with impact, so your prospect doesn't toss out your letter with all the other junk mail he receives.

SALES LETTERS WITH IMPACT

Suppose for a moment you're sitting at your desk and in walks a man you've never seen before. He tips his hat, greets you with a proper "Good morning," and says, "Valued customer, I wish to convey my company's deepest gratitude for the loyalty bestowed on us over the years and that we hope you will continue to show us in the future." You'd probably check your outer office to see if the little men in the white coats had accidentally misplaced this nut. Then, you'd simply toss him out the door.

Same with a sales letter that uses such archaic lingo. Yet, for some odd reason, people think this stilted language adds dignity and prestige to an otherwise crass sales pitch. Maybe it did 30 years ago. But not today. Today, it conjures up images of clerks with green eye shades and sleeve garters. Probably not the image your firm wishes to present.

If you have something to say—and you do or you wouldn't have written the letter in the first place—say it straight out, simply and to the point. Skip the rhetorical sludge.

Most business letters are written for one of three reasons: to request information, to provide information, or to sell. The first two are easy. "Please forward information regarding your new line of gimcracks . . ." or "This responds to your request regarding case discounts on gewgaws . . . ."

But a sales letter doesn't have to be difficult if you follow a few simple guidelines. Over the years of writing sales letters, and teaching others how to write them, I have evolved a four-step process (and a corollary) that, if followed, can make writing sales letters easier for you and profitable for your company.

Step #1: Grab their attention

Just as the headline of an ad should pull in the reader, so should the opening of your sales letter. It may
be a catchy first line, an enclosure, a striking layout,
or even an attractive envelope. This doesn't mean
you have to spend a lot of money. You simply need a
little, good old-fashioned ingenuity. Try these ideas:

- Have your printer crop one corner of your letter. Then open with: "If you find our competition is cutting corners on service, try our five-
  year service warranty on all parts and labor . . . ."
  Or "Trying to cut corners to make ends meet?
  Why not call us for a loan. . . ."

- Try a handwritten letter. Have your printer use blue ink on yellow blue-lined paper. (Be sure to use someone in your office with legible handwriting if yours, like mine, resembles the footprints of a gaggle of drunken pigeons wandering along the page.) Your message will stand out from the hundreds of neatly typed letters received daily. If you write it in a casual tone, you convey an intimacy sure to be an attention grabber.

  - Juggle the flow. To make a partic-
    ular point, indent a few lines.

Make one paragraph flush left, the next flush right.
Use bullets to make a series of points. Keep the
reader's eye moving.

- Begin with a story, or a problem you need help solving. Like this: "Help! We're drowning in excess inventory and need to make room for next year's models . . . ."

- Use humor. Here's one of my favorites:

  Help! Please save my home life by reading the enclosed catalog.

  My husband has been slaving over it night and day, working like a dog and treating me like one in the process. If it's not a smashing success, can you imagine what it will be like to live with him?

  So won't you please read Joe's catalog? It contains all sorts of new products designed to make your life easier (and mine, too).

  Sincerely,

  Judy Dokes (Joe's wife)

  Notice the catchy opening line. The reader immediately wonders how reading a catalog can save someone's home life. The number of personal notes to Judy that show up with your orders will attest to the effectiveness of this approach.

- Gadgets grab attention. Paste a little plastic computer on the page to announce your new Web site. Or enclose a key (who can ever throw one of those away?) that your prospect must bring to your business to see if it opens a special box to win a prize. By the way, it's a great way to get customers to show up at your trade-show booth, too. Contact your local sales promotion and premium merchandising specialists and get on their mailing lists. Their catalogs are likely to generate all sorts of attention-grabbing ideas.

Step #2: Get to the point

Tell 'em what they need to know and tell 'em fast. They may not read all the way down to paragraph seven to find out they can save hundreds of dollars by ordering before the end of the month. Put the primary benefit, the main reason they should buy from you, and buy from you now, in that first paragraph. You may not get another chance to hook 'em.

One of my favorite ploys for improving any sales letter is to cut off that first chit-chatty paragraph. Try it and see if it doesn't improve your next sales letter. Another trick: Move the last paragraph up front. The summary paragraph is often the best. Nail it on top, where your reader won't miss it.

(One caveat: If you're selling internationally, pay heed to the business customs of your buyer's home country. It's considered boorish in international circles to plunge into crass commercial discussions immediately. So, if you're selling internationally, use that first paragraph as a lead-in, but make it provocative enough to get your reader to read the next paragraph, where you're back to being crass and commercial.)

Step #3: The rationale

Give your customers a reason to buy. Better yet, give two or three. This is your sales pitch, the one you'd make if you were standing on the other side of his or her desk. Use lots of facts. The more facts you tell, the more you sell.

Use a list. They're easy to read and add eye appeal. For example:

Our new gizmos

- save you money;
- last longer;
- are incredibly convenient;
- make life easier for Judy and me (see above).

Use testimonials, the next-best thing to word-of-mouth advertising. Your customers will find it easier to believe the endorsement of a fellow customer over the puffery of the letter writer.

Step #4: Tell 'em where and when to buy
If your prospect puts down your letter before ordering, you're through. You must get him to act now!

Give a cut-off date, or some imposed limitation to force him to act now! If he feels he might miss out on a great opportunity, he's more likely to respond. "Order now, because this is a limited offer good only until . . ." works surprisingly well, if the reason for the cut-off is compelling, or even humorous. For instance, "My mom wants to use the warehouse for her next Mah Jong Club meeting, so we need to clear everything out by next week!" That kind of personal touch often works better than, "Offer good through August 15th" (when we plan on having an even bigger sale?).

Corollary: Always use a postscript.
Research shows that the familiar "P.S." at the end of a letter is read about three times as frequently as the body copy. So use the postscript to make your point one more time.

A few more tips
- Skip the fancy colors unless you have a very imaginative idea or other compelling reason. Paper stock and ink colors add to the cost of a sales letter and generally don't contribute much. Spend less on creative production and more on creative thinking.

- Skip the salutation unless you can personalize each letter using modern computer database techniques. Nothing turns off a prospective customer quicker than "Dear Sir;" (especially if she's a woman), or "Dear valued customer." How valuable will they feel if you don't even know their name?

- Lighten up. Everyone enjoys a good laugh, and humor sells. But keep it clean. Don't risk being offensive.

- Home readers need more persuasion than office readers. The purchasing agent who will sign an order in a heartbeat for thousands of his company's dollars will agonize for days at his home over a $150 lawn mower. Brevity to the office, where the pace is frenetic and the workload onerous. Long copy, with plenty of facts, to the home, where the tempo is more relaxed.

P.S. Follow these simple steps to make your sales letters more compelling, readable, and useful for your customers. Most important, they will generate more sales for your company.

MAILING LISTS

Now you have a forceful, compelling sales letter. Who do you send it to? From the day you open your business, begin compiling a list of your customers. No matter whether you are in heavy industrial equipment or retail sales, make a list.

Have a sign-up book in your store. Ask your sales people for names of customers. Glean names from trade publications. Add potential customers by recording all the business cards you pick up at trade shows and conventions.

Guard that list like the gold it represents. Keep it up to date. Then, use it. Keep your name in front of your customers and prospects on a regular basis. Use any excuse: a special sales event, holiday greeting, or my personal favorite, the newsletter. Eventually, excuses won't be necessary. Mailings will be a natural part of your business routine.

Make Money from Your Mailing List

You may even be able to turn your mailing list into cash. If you have a large enough list, with specific names and current addresses, you may be able to rent it to others.

Our company had the names, addresses, telephone numbers, even the height and weight of scores of men and women attending nursing school throughout the country. This was a list of soon-to-be upwardly mobile, home-establishing medical professionals.

We contacted list brokers to see if they had customers for our list. Boy did they ever. Credit card companies, insurance brokers, car-rental firms, furniture-rental firms, you name it. Lots of companies wanted to sell to them. We made about ten cents per name, and the broker made a percentage when he sold the list. Even though we had only a few thousand names, the same lists were sold over and over again. Great effort was made to keep this list current because it represented a valuable asset to our firm. Though we were in the business of manufacturing uniforms, we made a tidy profit selling the names of our customers to others.

Mailing lists might just create a whole new profit center for your company, too.

MERCHANDISING AND POINT-OF-PURCHASE SELLING

Hunting and farming for sales can occur right at your place of business, especially if you sell at retail. Think of your store as a battleground. Every inch of floor, wall, and counter space is contested savagely by hundreds of manufacturers, wholesalers, and distributors. This is the final proving ground. Will your customer buy your products? Or will she walk away?

If you're a retail-store operator, it's up to you. How effectively you display your wares may be the difference between winning and losing the battle for your bottom line. The Point-of-Purchase Advertising Institute claims that two thirds of all buying decisions are made right in the place of business. Even if that figure seems a little lofty, retailers should take the use of in-store signs and displays seriously. Here are a few helpful tips on maximizing sales at your store.

Signs
Signs serve as silent sales people. They never complain about being overworked, and they don't get paid a commission, either. They give product infor-

mation, demonstrate features, reinforce your advertising campaign, announce discounts, and actually generate sales all by themselves.

Use persuasive language on your signs. Studies show that key words draw customers: YOU, EASY, SAVE, NEW, ANNOUNCING, GUARANTEED, FREE, NOW, SALE. Not terribly innovative, but they work. A huge banner proclaiming SALE! or FREE GIFT! or SAVE 40%! will convince shoppers that they should buy from you right now.

Crucial to success: Keep it simple. Use clear lettering, no fancy script. Short phrases. No commas or periods. Exclamation points are good! (But not too many!!!)

Advertising Tie-ins
In-store signs and displays should tie in as directly as possible with your advertising, or your customers may become confused. Your ads leave a subliminal impression on your customers. Signs are useful to awaken the memory of those ads and help lead to a sale. If your signs and displays are consistent with your overall creative strategy, your customers' willingness to buy will increase.

One sure way to maintain consistency with your advertising is to blow up your ad into a five-foot-high poster, mount it, and display it in your window. Display smaller versions throughout your store. It's a smart way to ensure that your interior signs and displays tie in with your advertising. Simple, effective, and inexpensive. A winning combination.

Cross Merchandising
Group similar items together. In a hardware store, the plumbing fittings should not be mixed in with the electrical items or the paint supplies. If yours is a hobby store, all the model trains and accessories should be in one area of the store, all the radio-con-

trolled cars in another. If a person comes in to buy a railroad engine and sees several new city scenery displays (with a sign saying: "NEW! ON SALE! 30% OFF!"), you may pick up additional sales.

Sometimes a manufacturer may offer elaborate displays for use in your store. When laying in new stock, ask the manufacturer if point-of-purchase materials are available. Most are happy to comply. They may be able to provide you with banners, brochures, counter cards, display racks, signs, posters, and more. All you have to do is ask.

Vertical Displays, Not Horizontal

Too often retailers will place a whole line of products horizontally (in rows) across a display case, hoping to impress shoppers with their variety of styles and sizes of one particular item. Bad idea. Always display vertically. Line up similar items top to bottom. Shoppers' eyes will typically scan shelves left to right at eye level and see your vast assortment of items (all grouped together, of course, with similar types—see "Cross Merchandising"). You increase your chances of snagging their eyes (and their wallets) tenfold.

Let Them Touch

We humans judge the world using five senses. While sight is the most used, touch is the second most important when making a purchase decision. What does the plastic (or cloth or wood) feel like? Are the edges rough or smooth? How heavy is it?

Items under lock and key discourage buying. Shoppers are reluctant to bother a sales person to open a locked display case. Or they may simply not be willing to wait until the sales person is available. Unless it's easily pocketed and worth a fortune (jewelry, for example), keep it in the open. The increase in profit from additional sales will more than offset the loss from pilferage.

Organize

What's more dreary looking than a half-empty, dusty display? Or more wasteful than empty shelves that could be featuring and selling your best items?

Keep it clean. Nothing is less appealing than dust and dirt on merchandise. It discourages touching (see page 105). And it tells your customers you don't care about them. Restock your shelves regularly. Bare shelves, empty item hooks, and vacant display cases spell out-of-stock to your buyers. If they can't find what they're looking for right away, shoppers assume it was on the empty hook, or the vacant shelf. And you lose a sale.

Hook Them One Last Time

Make the check-out counter the most attractive place in your store. After all, it's your last chance to sell. Put the handy necessities by the cash register. In a hair salon, it's the shampoo and hair brushes. If you operate a drug store, film, batteries and other accessory items make for great impulse purchases.

Let your customers know they have options when paying. Always display credit card logos prominently, both in your window and at the cash register.

In the battle for customers, you need all the ammunition you can muster. Follow these few simple merchandising techniques and make your store a more pleasant place to shop, a more pleasant place to work, and a more pleasant place to count your profits at the end of the month.

Inexpensive marketing tactics that work

Big companies have big budgets and build their businesses using big tactics. But most small companies don't have deep pockets they can pick when they need to spend money for marketing. If yours is one of those companies that needs to achieve stellar results on a down-to-earth budget, here are a few low-cost tactics that are easy to implement and that offer surprisingly strong returns.

BUSINESS CARDS

Give every employee a business card with his or her name on it. Every employee. They will feel appreciated and take great pride in distributing them. The cards are inexpensive, and each one represents another opportunity for your name to be seen.

COLLATERAL MATERIAL

Collateral material is defined as "all that other cool stuff" you get when you spend money on advertising or promotion. When you make a significant purchase of media space, say six quarter-page ads in your industry trade magazine, you may have leverage to wheel and deal for extras. Start with rate discounts; always get the best deal you can. Then ask for a few "freebies." Like reprints—maybe a decorative one in brass for your wall. How about a poster-size blowup of your ad for your retail store or your company lobby? Or maybe a couple hundred copies for mailings? Radio and TV stations often have tickets to sporting events. Ask for two in the media's private stadium box. You can use them to entertain a key customer.

Even if you aren't making a significant purchase, most media will offer perks to new accounts. Check the trade magazines serving your industry. Every good trade magazine has a merchandising department. In it are hardworking individuals devoted to producing materials to promote the goods advertised in their pages. Their cooperation is boundless and inexpensive. Reprints, preprints, mailing lists, newsletter listings, presentations to industry buyers, trade show promotions—ask for them all.

DOOR HANGERS

They work. I know that sounds incredible. But they do. Door hangers range from the inexpensive black-and-white variety to 4-color mini-brochures. High school kids can blanket a neighborhood in an afternoon.

They're intrusive. They're inexpensive. They reach prospects in their homes. They allow you to choose your customers geographically, literally block by block. They have no surrounding competition unlike direct mail that gets lost among the other mail, or your newspaper ad that has to compete with all the other ads. Door hangers get noticed.

Quick, inexpensive, and profitable. Go figure.

FORMS

Company forms make powerful marketing tools. Every piece of corporate printing is a potential marketing vehicle. Each should carry the corporate message. Invoices, order forms, and order acknowledgments sent to customers and suppliers are another opportunity to implant your corporate logo, slogan, or even corporate mission statement in the minds of those you need to reach most.

Don't forget internal communications. Imprint sales forms, time sheets, and memo pads with your company logo, slogan, or mission statement. It creates *esprit de corps* and reminds employees of your firm's guiding principles.

ON-HOLD COMMERCIALS

People call your business every day. Unfortunately, some get put on hold. You can keep them waiting in silence. Or you can plug them into a local radio station and take the chance of having your customers hear a competitor's ad. They may even hang up and call the competitor.

Or you can market to this captive audience. When callers must be put on hold, play appropriate music in between messages about your products or services. For example, if you're a bank, communicate your latest CD rate; a car dealership, brag about your low prices; a health-care provider, explain the benefits of your services. Update the recordings as frequently as necessary.

A local recording studio can select suitable music for you, create the customized script, produce finished sound tracks, and furnish the endless-loop tape and player for considerably less than you might expect.

CUSTOMER QUESTIONNAIRE

Research says that two-thirds of customers leave a supplier because they think that supplier doesn't care about them, doesn't respond to their needs. Don't let this happen to you. Periodically, ask your customers, "How are we doing?" Make it easy for them to respond by providing a stamped, self-addressed envelope.

A questionnaire serves several purposes. It identifies trends, pinpoints problem areas, and may even lead to a new product or service that hadn't occurred to you before.

A recording studio distributed self-addressed questionnaires to all its customers for just three months. Among other things, it learned that customers wanted lower rates and longer hours. Based on its customers' input, the studio decided to extend its hours into the evening with "off-hour" rates. This better leveraged its capital equipment and increased revenue.

A Sample Questionnaire

How are we doing?
We can do better. Just tell us how.
Please take a moment to full out this questionnaire and return it. Postage is on us.
Thanks, from the staff at CPI.

	great	good	fair	poor
Speed	☐	☐	☐	☐
Creative Input	☐	☐	☐	☐
Quality	☐	☐	☐	☐
Courtesy	☐	☐	☐	☐
Price	☐	☐	☐	☐
Follow-up				
Dubs	☐	☐	☐	☐
Packaging	☐	☐	☐	☐
Billing	☐	☐	☐	☐

Suggestions/Comments _____

_____
_____

The reverse side of this simple postcard questionnaire had the company's return address and a stamp.

SPONSOR A LITTLE LEAGUE TEAM

Or a bowling team. Or sponsor a hole at a charity golf outing. Better yet, do all three. Be a part of the community in which you live and work. The benefits are not altogether altruistic. If you sell to local customers, team uniforms with your name on them are just one more way to create awareness for your company. Further, the goodwill you generate in your community will make it easier to hire good employees. Best of all, you have the satisfaction of knowing you support a good cause.

UNIFORMS

Mention uniforms to your employees and they conjure up images of orange polyester jumpsuits with "Judy" or "Norm" over the pocket. Pretty grim. But consider, uniforms can be everything from simple T-shirts to high fashion bought at the trendiest boutique. As long as they're "uniform."

Simply choose your corporate "style" and take your clothes to an embroiderer (listed in your local Yellow Pages). Spend a setup charge of $100 to $150 to make your company's name and logo (It's not your employee's name you want over the pocket. It's yours!); then each shirt, jacket, or baseball cap can be embroidered for about $5.

Research shows uniforms work in the workplace. The American public favors the idea of employees wearing identifiable apparel almost 8 to 1, according to a study conducted for the National Association of Uniform Manufacturers and Distributors (NAUMD).

Attribute	% Mentioning
Easier to recognize	97
More professional	73
More neat	69
More pride in their company	66
Better trained	58
More predictable	53

Whether yours is a machine shop where heavy-duty uniforms are worn to withstand dirt and frequent laundering or a financial institution where more formal attire is standard, uniforms appeal to customers.

Now maybe I'm a little prejudiced. After all, I operated an apparel firm specializing in uniforms. But it makes sense. This is a win-win tactic. Your employees get an attractive fringe benefit; you get a lot of good advertising. How? Use your staff as walking billboards. Put your logo on baseball caps, T-shirts, jackets, golf shirts, the latest in casual wear, or any kind of clothes your staff likes enough to wear outside their homes. Best advice: Let the employees pick their own "look" (within cost and style limits).

Even if your company name never evokes its own branded lifestyle like Harley-Davidson (which has acquired almost a cult following with its logo emblazoned on everything from jackets and T-shirts to suspenders and sleepwear), the benefits of name awareness alone are enormous. Maybe the motorcycle look is not for you. Or maybe you and your employees have to wear Brooks Brothers regularly. If so, a good-quality casual shirt or a 100-percent cotton sweater with the company crest tastefully embroidered on breast, collar, or cuff may be just the thing. Stylish apparel will be worn proudly outside the office, among your employees' friends and families, as well as at company-sponsored events (trade shows, golf outings, supplier appreciation dinners, etc.).

A client whose computer programmers frequently spent many consecutive days in their customers' offices was having trouble enforcing a dress code. The programmers, a creative and somewhat eccentric lot, often expressed their creativity (and eccentricity) in their manner of dress. Appearance was important to their credibility. Because the customers' computer departments usually have casual dress codes, we shopped a few different catalogs and outfitted all the programmers in khaki slacks and jean shirts with the company logo on the breast pocket. They looked sharp. My client gave each employee three shirts and two pairs of slacks and sold additional pieces to them at cost. Both customers and employees responded so favorably that a few months later we added cold weather dark slacks, some attractive sweaters, and several other outfits (naturally, with the company logo on the breast) to our "catalog." At the holidays, all the employees received a lined jacket with the company logo prominently displayed across their shoulder blades. The employees wore their comfortable but attractive clothing at work and play, and name awareness in their sales region increased dramatically.

Uniforms provide you one more way to get your name in front of your customers. Your employees appreciate the fringe benefit. And you're assured they always look sharp.

13
Tricks of the trade show

There are more than 5,600 trade shows, conventions, and expositions in the United States every year. Nearly every industry has a major trade show. And many local trade associations sponsor smaller regional shows, too.

Sometimes, it may seem as if you've been to every one of them. Slogging your way past booth after booth of blandly smiling men and women ready to tell you more than you ever wanted to know about their product or service. But despite sore feet, drudgery, and occasional boredom, trade shows can be an extremely valuable promotional tool and source of industry information. At a trade show, you can

- See new products and industry innovations, and show off your own new products or services
- Meet and greet prospective customers face to face
- Secure leads that you can follow-up later
- Develop names for your mailing list
- Socialize with buyers on an informal basis

As beneficial as they are, trade shows can also be expensive when you include the cost of the space, transportation, lodging, and the display itself. (Don't forget the "opportunity cost" of your sales staff's down time.) Industry behemoths spend fortunes on designing, building, and promoting their trade show booths. You can't afford to. With a little planning, you can develop a cost-efficient display and attract the most possible traffic to your booth.

BUILDING YOUR BOOTH

Start with the display. There are three basic types:

1. Custom design
2. Stock display
3. Self-contained unit

The custom designed unit is as simple or as elaborate as you want to make it and usually the most expensive. It's shipped to the show in a wooden crate, which must be opened, removed, and returned when it's time to pack up. This duty is performed by extortionists disguised as exhibit personnel. Expect to grease their palms with cold cash if you want your crate delivered promptly. So you not only have to pay for a custom-designed display, you also have to pay for the upkeep.

The stock display offers many of the benefits of a custom unit without the cost. Display houses will customize one of their stock displays with your company name and logo, paint it in your company colors, and add lights wherever you want. Some stock units come in modular sections. You can add or subtract sections to fit any exhibit space.

The self-contained unit is the least expensive display. A small unit can be carried by one person and set up inside a half hour. It's prefabricated and looks a lot like every other prefab display at the show. Some customization is possible, but often looks tacked on rather than part of the display.

Whichever display type you choose, maximize your trade show experience by making your booth stand out amid the seemingly vast banality of like displays. What makes one booth more appealing than the next? What draws qualified prospects to your booth?

ATTRACTING TRAFFIC TO YOUR BOOTH

You've spent a fortune preparing samples and printing up literature, you've sent invitations to all your customers and prospects, your sales staff is primed and ready to smile and bob their heads like so many ceramic dogs on the back ledge of a '78 Impala. And nobody shows up. No one stops by your booth. Why? Because they don't see it. Its drab decor is obscured by all the glitz and glamour of the booths around it.

You can't convert prospects into buyers unless you first convert browsers into prospects. There are a number of ways to get your booth noticed amid the chaos of color around you. First and foremost: Add eye appeal. Colorful displays. Blinking lights. Things that move. We used a simple revolving mannequin wearing one of our snazzier uniforms to attract booth browsers. The simple movement grabbed attention. Then, our sales staff went to work once the browser stopped at our booth.

Pique their curiosity. Use BIG **bold** letters across the front of your booth to ask a provocative question. "How many tons of sand does it take to forge one Acme Compression Tank?" This technique makes browsers want to enter your booth area to learn the answer.

Or stage a contest. A browser fills out a form with name, company, and address (which you add to your database) to win a prize. "Guess how many stitches went into our model's uniform and WIN A COLOR TV!"

SOME "DO'S" AND "DON'TS"

Here are a few more suggestions that can help you draw more customers to your booth, and make them more likely to buy when they get there.

Do put whatever's new where everyone can see it.

After "Where's the bathroom?" the most frequent question at a trade show is "What's new?" After all, that's why most people go to trade shows—to see what's new in the industry. Make sure your latest innovation is right out front where your prospects and sales people can find it quickly.

Don't give away a free gift to everyone visiting your booth.

It attracts all the wrong people, the "booth beggars" who have no interest in your product or service. The aim of a promotion is to draw traffic, but selected traffic. What's the point in giving a gift to someone who has already found your booth?

Do offer a gift redeemable with coupon.

About a month before the show, do a mailing containing a gift certificate, "redeemable only at our booth." Then, offer something of modest value (a pearl-drop pendant on a gold chain is good — works for women, and as a gift for men's wives or daughters). Make each holder sign the coupon before redeeming the gift. This holds the prospect in the booth a bit longer, giving you time for a little sales pitch.

Don't distribute catalogs.

Trade show trash bins are loaded with thousands of dollars' worth of literature. People visiting a trade show booth feel they should walk away with something. It gives them a sense of accomplishment, makes them feel they are gathering trade information, the reason for attending the show in the first place. They fully intend to read the catalog when they return to their hotel room or office.

But while intentions are strong, arms are weak. It's tough enough dragging your body around a trade show all day without lugging 40 pounds of literature, too. So, most hit the trash bin long before they are read.

Do distribute literature.

Use inexpensive single-sheet throwaway material, such as circulars, envelope stuffers, or ad reprints. Offer to send catalogs to prospective customers. Have a batch of catalog return cards on hand, ready to be filled out. This gets you names and addresses of hot prospects to add to your database and allows them time to look around your booth while you are writing down the information.

Don't have too many "booth sitters" in your booth at once.

If there are seven or eight sales people in your booth, and traffic is slow, send a few out on break. Too many people in the booth ready to pounce on a prospective customer can be intimidating.

Don't let your sales people set up the booth.

First of all, it's tiring, and you want them fresh when the customers start rolling in. Second, they probably don't have any taste anyway, and the booth is apt to look pretty grim. Better to have someone back at the office with the talent, taste, and time draw up a diagram—a simple drawing of what goes where. It will save hours of work and aggravation and will ensure a tasteful, attractive display.

Do use islands and counters in your booth.

They add interest, help set off special items, and they allow you to make better use of your limited space.

Don't use plush furniture in your booth.

Sales people lounging around are a turnoff to prospective customers. Even browsers do not wish to break up a party and will frequently pass by the booth. Functional seating, yes. But not the kind that encourages lounging.

Do use carpeting at your booth.

It's useful for establishing boundaries and, when color-coordinated, can add a touch of class. Also, it's easy on the feet for your sales people and for potential customers who have walked far on cold, hard floors.

Don't eat or chew gum in the booth.

It looks unattractive and makes it difficult to converse with prospective customers.

Do wear a uniform.

It doesn't have to be silly or uncomfortable. But everyone working your booth should share a similar look, whether it's the same shirt and tie with matching slacks, or simply a cap with the company logo. Make it easy for your prospective customers to identify who's who. (See Chapter 12, Section on "Uniforms.")

Following these few basic suggestions can ensure you of a crowd at your booth, and a successful trade show for your firm.

How to
establish
14
your
marketing
budget

For thirteen chapters we've looked at designing effective marketing strategies, creating potent promotional materials, and planning shrewd media purchases. So how much is this all going to cost? How much should you spend on promoting your business?

It's an oft-asked question. The correct answer is: enough. How do you determine how much is enough? It depends. On your industry, on your competition, and what it is you wish to accomplish.

In general, there are two ways to determine your budget: one is the *percent-of-sales* and the other is the *objective-task* method.

PERCENT-OF-SALES METHOD

The percent-of-sales method requires determining your sales for the upcoming period and applying a set percent of that number to advertising and promotion. How do you know what percentage to use? One rule of thumb: Try and stay right around the industry average. Most industry trade associations publish an average promotion and advertising expenditure as a percent of sales.

For example, many business-to-business advertisers spend as little as 2 or 3 percent of sales on advertising. Most service businesses spend 5 or 6 percent. Retail firms spend far more, as much as 10 percent to 20 percent of sales. McDonald's spends up to 16 percent of gross sales on combined national and regional advertising and promotion.

An industry that is extremely status- or style-conscious may spend far more. A fashionable jeans manufacturer, for instance, might spend as much as 35 percent of sales on advertising. A perfume company might set its marketing budget at 50 percent of sales or more.

If you elect to use the percent-of-sales method, be sure to base your advertising and promotion budget upon future sales. Let's say your company has $3 million in sales now, but your industry is growing dramatically and you think you can be a $4 million company within the next year or so. If your industry spends 8 percent of sales on advertising, budget 8 percent of $4 million or $320,000 for advertising, not $240,000 (8 percent of $3 million).

There are always exceptions to any rule, and the percent-of-sales method is no exception. To increase your share of the market, you may need to spend a greater percent of sales than your competition. This is called "buying market share." It means you may have to spend far more than the usual percent of sales to promote your product.

Or if you want to introduce a new product or service, you can't simply budget a percent of sales. There aren't any sales yet. In that case, it's important to examine the total market for your new product or service and establish a reasonable goal for your share of that market. Then, use percent of sales to determine your base advertising and promotion budget.

But remember, this base is only a bare minimum. Since no one has heard of your new product yet, plan on spending a significant premium in order to create awareness. How much of a premium? A good rule of thumb: double your percent-of-sales budget in the introductory year.

OBJECTIVE-TASK METHOD

During the go-go '80s, many companies adopted "objective-task" or "zero-base" budgeting. The theory was, "To heck with past sales, what's it gonna take to get where we wanna go?" Today, the objective-task method is widely used and favored by academicians and many larger companies who possess the in-house talent to determine the needs and costs of each task.

To use this method, first establish your sales goals. Then, determine the tasks necessary to achieve those goals. Each promotional tool must be identified separately, then combined with others to determine an overall budget.

For instance, suppose a retail store with $1 million in annual revenue wants to increase sales by 10 percent. It is agreed that, to meet this objective, the store must increase awareness of its location to residents in a new area not currently served by the store. The store reviews its past advertising and promotion budget and decides to focus new direct mail and publicity efforts to this area. Tasks can then be set and a budget determined as follows:

	Prior Budget	New	Combined
• Radio advertising	$ 45,300		
• Newspaper advertising	35,200		
• Production costs	6,500		
• Direct mail (including production)		7,600	
• Localized publicity		4,100	
• Research	4,300		
• 10% reserve for contingencies	10,100	1,300	
Total	$101,400	$13,000	$114,400

One big drawback of the objective-task method is that it requires far more skill, judgment, and research in determining tasks than does percent-of-sales method. Your small company may not have the talent among your personnel to determine a budget using this method. And you may not have the time to devote to the task. The extra time and talent needed may be too great to make a commitment to this method.

If you do decide to go ahead, though, include at least 10 percent of your budget for contingencies. This allows you to monitor your promotion efforts throughout the year to see if the objectives are being met. Then, if they are not, or if they are being over-achieved, you can adjust the budget upward or downward within the limits of this contingency-reserve fund. The fund is also useful for meeting special circumstances, such as a change in demand, a need to counter a competitor's promotion, or to implement a new promotional tactic.

15 Summary

If you're the type of reader who turns to the last page to see how the story ends, you've quickly arrived at this final section. You've also missed the guts of the story, which is the meat of marketing.

Though marketing does not have to be difficult or mysterious, it is not reductive; it cannot be boiled down to a few glib and easy points or phrases. Marketing is an "attitude." An attitude of thought and creativity, strategies and tactics that require learning and practice. This is marketing in all its naked glory, the development of an attitude, a mindset, a way of thinking about your business. It is the message this book has tried to inspire.

If you have skipped to this chapter looking for an ending, I can only offer a beginning, a recap of the "attitude" of *Naked Marketing*. Here goes: Conduct some primary quantitative research at a 95-percent confidence level to determine demographics and psychographics of your target base within quintile subsets to optimize your objective task budget. Got that? Now, create a balanced mix of compelling promotions optimized by net revenue using media designed to penetrate all possible target markets for the least cost.

If you understood all that, you don't need this book. If it's a mystery to you, don't feel alone. The tendency to turn marketing into mystifying mumbo jumbo leaves many grasping for meaning.

Let's strip it down to the bare essentials. If you remember nothing else from this book, remember this: Marketing is the process of figuring out who your customers are and what they want so you can give it to them—better, faster, cheaper than your competitors. This is the heart of *Naked Marketing*.

There's an old marketing maxim that says "50 percent of all advertising is wasted." Don't believe it. It's a lot more than 50 percent. Traditional mass-media advertising is a monologue hoping to affect a passive audience. No wonder more than half of all advertising is wasted. It's amazing it's not more.

Imagine for a moment that fully half of all the television viewers who saw a Ford Motor Company commercial actually bought a Ford. Or, were even interested in buying a car at all. Imagine if McDonald's actually sold a cheeseburger to half the folks who watch each of their television commercials. It doesn't happen. Ford and McDonald's are huge companies with huge marketing budgets. They can afford the inefficiencies of mass-media advertising. If yours is a small business, you can't.

The secret is to know your customer. Segment your target as tightly as possible. Determine exactly who your customers are, both demographically and psychographically. Match your customer with your medium. Choose only those media that reach your potential customers, AND NO OTHERS. Reaching anyone else is waste.

For example, with the vast array of new media in the '90s, audience segmentation is easier than ever before. A syndicated cable television show may appeal to a limited niche, but it just may be a niche that is identical to your target. Trade magazines and hobby magazines appeal to very small groups of people of virtually every ethnic or lifestyle subdivision. Some direct sales and research services can even predict the buying habits of families city block by city block. And the Internet is viewed by anybody and everybody, from across the street and around the world, with news groups and search engines that can pinpoint your target audience in a cybersecond.

These media help small businesses like yours maximize every marketing dollar, firmly establish your market niche, and avoid that wasted 50 percent.

If you're *not* the type of reader to sneak a peak at the story's end and you've read this book, you should now have an understanding of this *process* of marketing. Research your customers; establish your identity; plan your marketing strategy; and implement tactics that will return the greatest net revenue.

That's it. The bare essentials. You now possess the basic tools to build your business.

And if it's true that 50 percent of all advertising is wasted, you've just improved the odds.

Glossary

Backward Channeling   Reversing the flow of materials through the distribution channel, with the consumer as producer. Recycling is an example of backward channeling. The consumer produces trash and recycles it "backward" through the distribution channel so that it can be made into useful products.

Blueprint   Term used in offset lithography to describe a photo-print used as a final proof. Always fold and assemble it to show how the finished printed piece will look. See "Van Dyke"

Blurb   A brief commendatory publicity notice, as in a newspaper.

Body   The main portion of the layout or printed form, as opposed to the headline, sub-headings, photo caption, or tag line.

Boutique Agency   An advertising agency specializing in one, or perhaps two, of the five major functions of a full-service agency: media, research, graphic design, copywriting, or strategic planning.

Campaign   Similarity between one advertisement and another. This could mean the consistent use of the same spokesperson (the Maytag repairman), the same demonstration (a drop of Dawn Dishwashing Liquid dispersing grease), the same words

("American Express, don't leave home without it."), or the same sound (the musical percolator that advertised Maxwell House coffee). A good campaign uses a *big idea* that illustrates the key benefit. It possesses an *attitude* that becomes the personality of the brand.

Chromalin or Chromalin Proof   A facsimile of a full-color printed piece, created chemically (from chromium... hence, the name), used to determine the accuracy of colors in the printing process.

Collateral Material   All that other cool stuff you get when you spend money on advertising or promotion. The media sales reps offer collateral materials—reprints, posters, or baseball caps and other *free* gifts as incentives to choose their media.

Competitors   The bad guys. Other companies selling products or services inferior to yours that your customers are lured, cajoled, coerced, or otherwise tricked into buying instead of buying yours.

Creative Director   At an advertising agency, the person in charge of all aspects of the character and quality of the agency's work for its clients. The creative director's background is most frequently either copywriting or art direction.

Cross Merchandising   Displaying together those products that may be used together. Supermarkets place the peanut butter next to the jelly, the dip with the chips, the salad dressings in the produce section. Hobby retailers have all their model railroad trains and accessories in one area of the store.

Cyberspace   A medium of communication between computers. A New Age medium requiring new strategies and a new approach for marketers. See "World Wide Web"

Demographics   The statistical characteristics of human population, such as age, gender, race, religion, or income.

Doodad   A product. See "Gimcrack."

Early Adopters   The first wave of consumers for new products, these pioneers buy all the latest products simply because they are new.

Entrepreneur   An individual with enough skill, audacity, and pluck to organize, manage, and assume the risks of a business enterprise.

Farming   Growing sales from existing customers.

Flighting   Concentrating your advertising into bursts, with a hiatus (no advertising) in between. In broadcast, you might run your ads for four weeks, then be off the air for four weeks before repeating the ads. In print, it's skipping an issue or two before running the ads again.

Forward Integration   A company seeking ownership of its distribution system. For example, a manufacturer may buy up (or start up) retail outlets for its products.

Four I's   The process of creativity: Information, Incubation, Inspiration, and Implementation.

Four P's   These are the marketing variables that influence the level of customer response. They include: Product, Place, Promotion, and Price. Each variable has several subvariables. Quality, features, name, and packaging are all Product variables. Discounts, credit terms, and allowances are all Price variables. And so on.

Frequency   The number of times your audience hears or sees your message, on average. Repetition aids retention, so frequency makes your message better remembered.

Front Loading   Spending the lion's share of your media budget in the early stages of your advertising campaign.

Gewgaw   A product. See "Doodad."

Gimcrack A product. See "Widget."

Gizmo A product. See "Gewgaw."

Gravure High-quality reproduction, usually on rotary presses (also called rotogravure). High cost of printing cylinders limits gravure to long runs, such as mail-order catalogs and Sunday supplements.

Gross Rating Points (GRP) Reach times frequency equals gross rating points (R × F = GRP). If your message is received in three out of five homes in your market, reach is 60; if each home receives your message an average of two times, the frequency is two. 60 × 2 = 120 GRPs.

Headline Embodies the main selling point of your advertisement. A headline is read five times more often than body copy.

Home Page The first page of your web site, the first one a user sees when visiting your company's address in cyberspace.

Hunting Increasing sales by finding new customers, rather than selling more product to existing customers.

Iambic Pentameter A form of writing consisting of five metrical feet, each foot having a short syllable followed by a long syllable, or one unstressed syllable followed by a stressed syllable. Used almost exclusively in all of William Shakespeare's writings.

Image Perception of your product or company among former, current, and future customers, employees, vendors, and the general business community.

Internet A medium of communication between computers. A New Age medium requiring new strategies and a new approach for marketers. See "World Wide Web"

Late Adopters Cautious consumers who don't buy new products simply because they are new.

Layout A rough sketch of what the advertisement will look like. Sometimes called a *thumbnail* sketch. After approval at this stage, a more comprehensive layout, called a *comp*, will be prepared.

Letterpress Oldest and most versatile method of printing, allowing changes up to the last moment. Used most often by newspapers and some magazines.

Lithography Often called *offset* because the image is first printed on a rubber roll, then offset onto paper. Combination of good quality and low plate costs makes it attractive for many magazines.

Marketing The satisfaction of needs and wants through the sale of your products or services.

Mechanical Final assembly of the illustration, headline, and body copy prior to printing.

Mission Statement Defining your business in terms of your customers, your employees, and your business philosophy. The statement answers the question: "Why am I in business?"

Mystique An air or attitude of mystery and reverence surrounding something. The bewilderment caused by marketing *gurus* unable to explain the fundamentals of their craft.

Name Awareness The ability to achieve top-of-mind response among your target customers. When asked which brand comes to mind in your product category, prospects name your product first.

Net Revenue Projection The profit (or loss) projection of each tactic. Derived by deducting cost of goods and the cost of the tactic from the estimated additional revenue the tactic will generate.

Objective Task   One method of determining your marketing budget. Define the marketing objectives, assign the tasks necessary to achieve the objectives, and sum the costs of the tasks.

Percent of Sales   The other method of determining your marketing budget. Determine sales for a given period (usually one year) and assign a percent of sales to marketing.

Point of Purchase (POP)   Promotion material placed on, at, or in retail stores. May include banners, posters, streamers, displays, signs, or racks. Any advertising material at the point where the purchase is made.

Post-Purchase Preference   The consumer's level of satisfaction or dissatisfaction following the purchase of a product or service. Leading to brand preference. Satisfaction is a function of expectations and the product's perceived performance. If product performance meets or exceeds expectations, the customer will prefer the product when making future purchases.

Post Script   A brief sentence or two appended to a letter or article. Usually read more frequently than the body of the letter itself.

Primary Research   Research performed by you, yourself. Research that cannot be found in the library, on the Internet, in books, magazines, or newspapers. In marketing, primary research consists principally of asking customers and prospects what they want. It may also include what they watch, what they read, what they listen to.

Publicity   Editorial copy in the media which, unlike advertising, has no cost. Because it is presented in the press as a story, it also has more credibility with viewers than paid advertising. See "Blurb"

Psychographics   The psychological factors that separate consumers. These include *lifestyle* and *personality* differences. People within the same demographic group can exhibit very different psychographic profiles. Terms such as yuppy, jet-setter, gay, and straight are all lifestyle descriptions. Marketers try to match lifestyle and personality when creating a brand image. For instance, Marlboro cigarettes appeal primarily to men who envision themselves independent "cowboy" personalities. Virginia Slims appeal principally to sophisticated women.

Q,S&P   Quality, Service, and Price. Successful companies determine which two out of these three they will offer their customers. High quality and exceptional service justifies a higher price. A low price is necessary whenever the quality is inferior or service is substandard. Any company that fails to offer at least two out of the three will soon be out of business. Likewise, any company that tries to offer all three will also soon be out of business.

Quintile Analysis   Categorizing five target markets (usually geographic areas) by sales volume: heavy users, higher-than-average users, average users, lower-than-average users, and nonusers. Quintile analysis of a beer brand may reveal heavy consumption in the South and Southeast, higher-than-average consumption in the Northeast, average consumption in the Midwest, lower-than-average consumption in the Southwest, and nonconsumption in the Northwest and West.

Reach   The number of different homes (or people) exposed to your advertising message. If your media plan "reaches" four out of every five homes, it has a *reach* of 80.

Screen   Formerly called silk screen because the printing stencil was made of silk. Provides brilliance and depth of color for short runs. Especially suited for billboards and transit advertising.

Secondary Research Using information compiled by others. An encyclopedia offers secondary research.

Segmentation The process of dividing your prospects and customers by demographic or psychographic criteria. For example, segmenting your target market by gender, frequency of use, and so on.

Suggestive Selling Suggesting additional items to current customers. Offering accessories, warranties, or service contracts when selling your primary product or service.

Target Audience Those persons with whom you most wish to make contact, your primary prospects. Your target may be defined demographically, psychographically, or both.

Target Rating Points (TRP) Reach times target percent times frequency equals target rating points ($R \times T\% \times F = TRP$). If your message is received in four out of five homes in your market, reach is 80; if just two out of every ten of those reached are your target audience, target percent is 20 percent; if each home receives your message an average of three times, the frequency is three. $80 \times 20\% \times 3 = 48$ TRPs.

Testimonials Testimony given by another person in praise or support of your product.

Theory X An authoritarian management approach where it is assumed employees dislike work and need firm direction and control.

Theory Y A management approach where it is assumed employees are more committed to the company and its mission if they participate in the decision-making process.

Theory Z A combination of Theories X and Y where employees are given attainable goals and asked to offer plans designed to achieve those goals.

Total Approach   A combination of image advertising and product advertising. Using consistent design elements, mood, or message in your advertising to create a brand image while promoting specific products.

Type   The style of lettering used in an advertisement. There are hundreds of type styles. Some have serifs, short lines on the tops and bottoms of letters. (This is a *serif* type style.) Other type styles are sans serif (This is *sans serif*).

Van Dyke   A photographic image, usually made on inexpensive photopaper, used as a proof from a negative. See "Blueprint"

Web Site   Your company's address in cyberspace where prospective customers can tap into your organization for information about your company and its products.

Widget   A product. See "Gizmo."

World Wide Web   That portion of the Internet used to display text, graphics, and video clips. Accessed through computers hooked by telephone line into the Internet, this relatively new medium offers a whole new means of marketing products to customers worldwide.

Index